I'M A LUCKY ONE

I'M A LUCKY ONE

BY S/Sgt Barry Sadler

with Tom Mahoney

THE MACMILLAN COMPANY, *New York*

COLLIER-MACMILLAN LTD., *London*

Library of Congress Catalog Card Number: 67–15666

JACKET PHOTOGRAPH COURTESY RCA VICTOR

FIRST PRINTING

The Macmillan Company, New York
Collier-Macmillan Canada Ltd., Toronto, Ontario

Contents

Illustrations Follow Page 96

I'M A LUCKY ONE

"I'm a Lucky One"

1 ON MEMORIAL DAY OF 1965, I lay in a bed in the United States Army's Eighth Field Hospital. This adjoined the airport at Nha Trang, a port city on the South China Sea that was Vietnam headquarters for our Special Forces, the wearers of the green beret. Nha Trang is 198 miles northeast of Saigon and in the days of French rule was a popular beach resort. The hospital's airport location made it easy to bring wounded there from the interior by helicopter and light plane and also to fly out of the country those hurt seriously, giving the wounded the highest survival rate of any war. I could see the planes from my window.

A few days earlier I had bumped into a *punji* stick in the tall grass of the Central Highlands while leading a patrol of native Montagnard tribesmen out of a camp southeast of Pleiku. These razor-sharp bamboo sticks covered with excrement were everywhere. Tax collectors of the enemy Viet Cong forced the natives to supply them by the hundreds. They varied in length, but the most common were of Tinkertoy size and hard to detect. As a Special Forces medic, I knew about them. But I had been taking an antibiotic because of a touch of dysentery, and the wound, in my left leg near the knee, seemed slight. I pulled the stick out, stuck in a cotton swab, tried to clean out the cut, put on an adhesive bandage, and finished the patrol. This was a mistake. My leg swelled with pain. I developed a massive infection. To drain it, surgeons enlarged the wound to a ten-inch gash.

They poured penicillin, millions and millions of units,

9

into me at the hospital via plastic intravenous tubing. I knew enough medicine to realize that possibly the future of my life and certainly that of my leg was riding with the penicillin. Mines, *punji* sticks, and booby traps are hard on legs in Vietnam.

I was mad. Except for three months between enlistments, I had been in first the Air Force and then the Army for seven years. Perhaps $100,000 had been spent on my training and education, but I had been laid low by the cheapest and most primitive of weapons. Would it be taps for me? I wondered whether I would see Lavona, my wife, and Thor, our little boy, again. I had asked her to keep Thor's name Sadler if I were killed and she remarried. She had promised, and this was some comfort to me as I worried in the hospital at Nha Trang.

While watching the straw-colored penicillin flow into me, I listened intermittently to a small radio set that somebody had in an adjoining bunk. This was tuned to a distant station broadcasting programs from America, some of them several days old. Vietnam is thirteen hours ahead of Eastern Standard Time. When it is noon in New York and Washington it is 1 A.M. the next day in Vietnam, but when it is midnight in New York it is 1 P.M. the same day in Vietnam. Very confusing.

Suddenly over the air and over the ocean came a voice speaking about the Special Forces. We turned up the set, and I listened intently.

". . . for the men of Special Forces," said the speaker, "are the men who go first; men who fight not in great battles that draw front-page attention but in places with strange, unknown names and sometimes no names at all; men who live in discomfort and hardship while their countrymen live in ease and happiness at home; men who fight and die in loneliness far away.

"You men of the Green Berets—you who wear what President Kennedy called 'a symbol of excellence, a badge of courage, a mark of distinction in the fight for freedom'— you know the special character of the dangers you face.

"In Vietnam alone, you have won more than four hundred Purple Hearts—as well as every other military decoration a grateful nation can bestow.

"Captain Donlon, who is here today, won the Medal of Honor. Two of his sergeants, who are with us only in spirit, won the Distinguished Service Cross. Four others of his team won Silver Stars, and five others won Bronze Stars with 'V' for 'Valor.' "

Captain Roger Hugh C. Donlon, from Saugerties, New York, was an officer of the Seventh Special Forces Group, to which I had been assigned for part of 1964. We were also both school dropouts. He had dropped out of West Point and made a comeback to win his parachutist's badge and captain's bars. He went to Vietnam as commander of an "A" team, A-726, which was sent to Camp Nam Dong, near both Laos and North Vietnam, as advisers to a force of three hundred South Vietnamese. When the Viet Cong struck before dawn, Captain Donlon was wounded in the stomach, leg, forearm, and shoulder but rallied the defense and beat off the attack in a five-hour battle, during which he killed many of the enemy himself. He recovered from his wounds in the Eighth Field Hospital and received from President Lyndon B. Johnson the first Medal of Honor awarded for action in Vietnam.

"This was a great team," continued the voice on the air, "but it was not an unusual team. I believe that any other Special Forces team in that situation would have shown the same dedication, the same heroism, and would have earned the same recognition.

"Courage is common in your ranks. You brought it here with you—as did Captain Lee Mize, who won the last Medal of Honor awarded in Korea—and you have shown it in every situation in which you have found yourselves since. But you give to your country more than courage. . . . You are meeting the challenge of our time. You are doing your duty—the duty to understand your world rather than simply fight for it.

"You fight what President Kennedy called 'another kind of war'—new in its intensity, ancient in its origin—war by guerrillas, subversives, insurgents, assassins; war by ambush instead of by combat, by infiltration instead of aggression, seeking victory by eroding and exhausting the enemy instead of engaging him. 'It requires,' he said, 'a wholly different kind of force.'

"Yours are the different kind of force. . . . Your equipment includes no atomic weapons, no tanks, not even heavy artillery. Instead there are medics who treat not just the wounds of battle but the many diseases of a tropical village; engineers whose knowledge is not limited to fortifications but extends to the building of schools, clinics, housing in areas where these things have never existed; soldiers who see their duty not in the destruction of people but in the destruction of the ignorance and disease and disorganization in which discontent and rebellion flourish.

"As Sergeant Major Francis Ruddy tells you, this new kind of war is won when a great battle results in the death of many enemies; it is won on the day when no one dies because your work has isolated the insurgents, stripped them of their support, and thus rendered them harmless."

The voice was that of Senator Robert Kennedy of New York, who was speaking at the dedication of the new John F. Kennedy Center for Special Warfare, named for his brother the late President Kennedy, at Fort Bragg, the home of the Green Berets. I was moved by the speech.

I had been fighting for months "in places with strange, unknown names and sometimes no names at all." I had become used to killing a cruel and ruthless enemy.

As a medic, I also had fought in the "other war," the effort to win the support of the natives. One day they brought me a very sick, bloated baby whose bowels had not moved for four days. I found a soft hollow reed, filled my mouth with soapy water, and gave the baby an enema that may have saved his life. There was more satisfaction in this than in the shooting.

For two years I had been trying to sell a song about the Special Forces in which I described our work and mission in words very like those of Senator Kennedy. It was then called "The Ballad of the Green Beret." I later made "Beret" plural. Some of the lines are:

> Silver wings upon their chests,
> These are men, America's best.
> One hundred men we'll test today,
> But only three win the Green Beret.

> Soldiers from the sky,
> Soldiers who fight and die,
> Men who mean just what they say,
> Hail the men of the Green Beret.

> Trained to live off nature's land,
> Trained to fight with their bare hands,
> Men who fight by night and day,
> Hail the men of the Green Beret.

The boys at Fort Bragg thought it was great, and at the suggestion of a fellow trooper I copyrighted it in 1963. A New York music company believed it looked promising. A lot of people had heard it, but it was still unpublished and unrecorded. I resolved that day to see that America heard my song, even if I had to give it away, if the penicillin did its work and I left the hospital. I also had a few more songs and at the moment was working on one saluting the green-uniformed nurses who were taking care of me in the Eighth Field Hospital at Nha Trang.

Lieutenant Colonel Margaret G. Clarke, a soft-spoken Alabama girl who had nursed soldiers for twenty-three years, arrived in Vietnam early in 1965 to be Chief Nurse at the Eighth Field Hospital and to head Army nursing in Vietnam. One of her previous patients had been President Eisenhower at Walter Reed Hospital. I had started right to work on the idea when she asked me, a few months earlier, to write a song about the American nurses in Vietnam. The first of these nurses, a group of thirteen, had arrived in March, 1962, and were assigned to Nha Trang. Vietnam's Army nurses have included many noble and notable women. Colonel Clarke's predecessor there, Major Mary D. Clark, was awarded the Army's Bronze Star Medal and the Air Force Commendation Medal. Captains Ruby N. Stanfield and Maryanne Dietrich and Lieutenants Catherine Schilling and Julie Klebaum all received medals for work at the Eighth Field Hospital. In their spare hours, some of these women helped in Vietnamese orphanages and hospitals. Colonel Clarke herself received the Legion of Merit and the Air Medal and later was chosen U.S. Army Nurse of the Year for 1965.

Four Navy nurses were hurt when a Viet Cong bomb exploded on Christmas Eve of 1964 in a Saigon hotel where they were quartered. They helped others and refused treatment themselves until all the other fifty-eight Americans and one Australian who had been hurt in the blast had had their wounds bandaged. These heroic women were Lieutenants Barbara J. H. Wooster and Ann Darby Reynolds of Dover, New Hampshire; Frances Lee Crumpton of Haleyville, Alabama; and Lieutenant Commander Ruth Ann Mason of Brooklyn, New York. The four nurses received the first Purple Hearts given women for injuries in the Vietnam conflict.

Our nurses in Vietnam deserved a song, all right. When I finished it, I sang it to my own guitar accompaniment and gave tapes of it to Colonel Clarke. She mailed them to the Chief of Nurses, but they never arrived. When the *punji* stick landed me back in her hospital, she asked me to do the song over. I did so and made more tapes. The song was called "Salute to the Nurses," and it recognized the male nurses, of which there are some in Vietnam, as well as the women nurses, with these lines:

After the battle, after the fight,
Many owe their lives to the ladies and men in white.

And all of the men in this war-torn land
Salute the nurses of Vietnam.

They know the awful toll of war each day,
They know more than any what price we pay.

A soldier, his hands too burned to write,
A nurse takes down his words through the lonely night.

They have gone to the front where men fought in the night,
From Pleiku to Kwinyon where war these men fight.

Many a wounded soldier's pain is eased for a while
*By opening his eyes to see a nurse's smile. . . .**

On the map, "Kwinyon" is "Qui Nhon," but it is hard to sing this way. It is the name of a smaller port city a

* Copyright © 1965 and 1966 by Music Music Music Inc.

hundred miles north of Nha Trang. Highway 19, the east-west road connecting Qui Nhon with Pleiku, the center of Special Forces activity in the Central Highlands, is probably the most frequently bombed and ambushed road in the whole country. But it has many rivals, and the war at times pops up in areas where it is least expected.

I was lying in my hospital bunk looking out the window the next evening, which was the last day of May or the first of June, when I noticed a bright light and heard a loud *whump*. Maybe an oil drum blowing up, I tried to tell myself. But the sound was unmistakably mortar fire. I looked out the window again and saw a helicopter blown up. The Viet Cong were shelling the Nha Trang airport.

Without hesitating, I pulled the IV tubes out of my arm. I was being given fluids as well as the penicillin. My slashed leg was in a cast, but I threw it over the side of the bed and went through the door fast.

"Where do you think you are going?" demanded a young nurse. She may have been Captain Hansine Jensen, a new girl from Montana who had been taking care of me.

"Outside, lady!" I shouted as I hobbled through the door. "Those are mortar rounds coming in, and they ain't ours!"

I ran outside, found me a hole, and waited for things to quiet down. When they did, I went back inside, attached the IV tubes, and went to sleep.

The next day I was evacuated to the Philippines. Before leaving, I gave Colonel Margaret Clarke a beaten-gold-

and-jade pendant that I had picked up from the natives in the Highlands and also a Montagnard sword, the kind they use for head-lopping. It was really just a glorified machete but quite ornate. I liked Colonel Clarke very much. She had been good to me, as she was to scores of others, regardless of rank. She ran a fine hospital. It was soon expanded from one hundred beds to four hundred beds. Surgery sometimes went on twenty-four hours a day.

I carried my guitar and gear aboard a C-119 cargo plane that had been fitted by the Military Air Transport Service for carrying litter cases. A few hours later, we touched down at Clark Air Force Base, sixty miles northwest of Manila. The place is named for Major Harold M. Clark, who was killed in 1920 in an accident over the field.

Air Force doctors took charge of me at the Clark Field Hospital. My leg was no worse but also no better. The penicillin and the *punji* infection seemed to be fighting a draw. The doctors kept the wound open and draining for several days. They then closed it with wire sutures. Two of them had a bet as to whether these would hold, because the gash had become three inches wide. It was hard to make the skin stretch that far. Fortunately it held. I was told the chances were my leg would be all right but would be stiff for a long time.

On the strength of this, I wrote my wife, Lavona, that there was a chance that I might be coming home. She and our young son were then with her family in Lehighton, Pennsylvania. Until then, like seventy-five percent of the soldiers wounded in Vietnam, I had told her nothing about being hurt and had asked the hospitals to say nothing. It was several days before the hospital doctors decided what to do with me.

"Sergeant Sadler," an Air Force captain finally told me one morning, "you are going home. You're a lucky one."

Inspired by his words, I wrote in a few minutes what I thought my best song since composing and taping the then unpublished "Ballad of the Green Berets." Titled "I'm a Lucky One," from the Air force doctor's sentence, it paid tribute to the memory of three Special Forces sergeants, all friends of mine, who had been killed in Vietnam. They were Raymond J. Vrba, Jr., of Stedman, North Carolina; Horace E. Young of Aledo, Illinois; and Emmett H. Horn of Vidor, Texas. I played the song around the hospital while awaiting transportation to the United States. The words came out like this:

> I'm goin' home, my tour is done.
> I'm goin' home, I'm a lucky one.
>
> But I've left friends behind me
> Who won't come home no more,
> Yes, many friends remain forever on that bloody shore.
> But at night when I sleep
> I know my dreams will be about my friends
> I left across the sea.
>
> I'll hear Vrba, Young, and Horn laugh again out loud.
> We'll all be together in a happy crowd.
>
> But then I hear the sound of bullets whining overhead,
> Feel the crash of mortars, and all my friends are dead.

My friends they fought and gave their all,
My friends they died for freedom's call.

As my dream is ending, they'll come and say good-bye.
Tho' I'm sound asleep, a tear I'll cry.

And they say something that fills my heart with pain:
Tell them about us, Sadler,
*Don't let us die in vain.**

This is what I have tried to do with my songs. This is what I am trying to do in these pages.

* Copyright © 1965 and 1966 by Music Music Music Inc.

Reveille

2 NEW SOLDIERS fight with new weapons, but at many posts and bases soldiers wake up and move through their days to the stirring notes of old bugle calls. Even when it is only a recording played over a public-address system, a bugle call lifts the heart and tingles the spine in a way that neither squawk-box command nor buzzer can do.

I heard reveille for the first time in June, 1958, at 5 A.M. at Lackland Air Force Base, just west of San Antonio, Texas. Reveille is an old French call. It may have been heard by Joan of Arc. The bugle call retreat is inherited from the Crusades. Mess call and assembly are old too. Tattoo dates from the seventeenth century and the Thirty Years' War in Germany. Originally "taptoo," it told tavern keepers to turn off their beer taps and soldiers to go to their quarters.

Generals since Julius Caesar have recognized the value of music and song for fighting men. Music can inspire and encourage the soldier and help him forget that he is lonely, weary, and far from home. Shakespeare says that the man who has no music in himself and is not moved by it "is fit for treasons, stratagems, and spoils." Foot soldiers can march nearly twice as far in a day with music as they can without it. The ancient Romans had a tuba player in every company. History says that the 42nd Highlanders, ordered by Wellington to play their bagpipes as they never had before, turned the tide for the British at Waterloo. A poet has written that three men "with a new song's measure can trample an empire down."

I wasn't ready for anything so ambitious when the notes of reveille struck my ears for the first time that June morning in a Lackland barracks. The notes were clear, but my head was not. A lot of men were running around naked. I wondered for a moment whether I was in jail. My immediate problem was to get from an upper-tier bunk to the floor. A lot had happened to me in the previous twenty-four hours, the major event being that the day before in Denver, several hundred miles away, along with a score of young men, nearly all older than my seventeen years, I had raised my right hand and repeated: "I, Barry Allen Sadler, do solemnly swear that I will bear true faith and allegiance to the United States of America; that I will serve them honestly and faithfully against all their enemies whomsoever; and that I will obey the orders of the President of the United States and the orders of the officers appointed over me according to regulations and the Uniform Code of Military Justice."

If you volunteer for the armed services, you have a lot of choices. My first thought had been to enlist in the Navy, but the other services have a "buddy" plan of enlistment. Under this, which is formally the Buddy Basic Training Plan, two to five friends from the same community who want to enlist and stay together are assured of being assigned to the same post, the same unit, and even of going on leave at the same time. This is definite only for the eight weeks of basic training, during which many a soldier feels he needs a friend. If buddies are equally qualified and interested in the same service specialty, there is a good chance that they will continue in the same outfit and may go overseas together.

I had a buddy in Leadville, Colorado, named Delfino Gomez, a skinny, thoughtful, curly-haired guy. We had gone to high school together there. He was slightly older than I and had done better in classes. He was next to the oldest of ten children in his family. His father worked in the smelter, and Delfino was a hotel bellboy. We were both from the wrong side of the tracks, had been in all sorts of scrapes together, and liked each other a lot. He was always ready to help me, with no questons asked. He was my closest, almost my only friend. He thought we should go into the Air Force and the "wild blue yonder." An Air Force recruiter in Leadville also was persuasive.

"All right," I agreed, "we'll go into the Air Force on the buddy system."

I got my mother's permission to volunteer. This is required if you are under eighteen. But at the last minute, Delfino decided he was needed too much at home and backed out. Three years or so later, he went into the Army and made a good soldier. As this is written, I believe he is chief clerk at a field hospital on Okinawa in the Pacific.

I went ahead to Denver and the swearing-in ceremony without Delfino, but his change of mind had shaken me considerably. To fortify myself against what seemed an uncertain future, I felt obliged to bring along a jug of tequila, the strong cactus-distilled drink of Mexico and the Southwest. I hid this in my kit bag and sipped it as the old C-46 transport plane took us from Denver to San Antonio.

We flew over several places where I have lived. It was my first plane ride and also my first day in the Air Force. I got a little high.

As far as I know, I am the first soldier in my immediate family in three generations. But we are not a close family, so I may be wrong. We rarely write letters or make long-distance telephone calls and don't keep up with one another too well. Outside of my parents and elder brother, Robert, who is five years older than I am, the only members of the family I remember seeing as a boy were a couple of aunts, sisters of my mother. These were Aunt Hope, who is Mrs. Clyde Stockham of Phoenix, Arizona, and Aunt Joyce, who is Mrs. George Baker of Kingman, Arizona. They were kind to my brother and me.

The Sadlers are of German descent, I think, with a touch of Black Irish. The name at one time may have been Von Zadler. Some of them emigrated to Texas and then to Arizona. My father, John Sadler, and my mother, who was Bebe Littlefield before she married, were from Phoenix. When my mother was born, the leading movie actress was Bebe Daniels, and I have an idea this accounts for her given name. My father studied at Arizona State University in Tempe. Before I was born, they moved to New Mexico, where the automobile license plates carry the line "Land of Enchantment," and my father developed a successful plumbing and electrical business in Carlsbad. He also bought several farms in the neighborhood, including a twenty-acre one west of the city, in Happy Valley, on which I lived when I was a small boy. We planted tomatoes and vegetables, but some years the only crop was dust. My brother and I did some of the farm work. Dad worked hard himself and believed that everybody else should work.

The city was first called Eddy, after the cattlemen brothers who founded it, but when it was discovered that local springs contained the same minerals as water at Carlsbad, the famous spa in Czechoslovakia, that name was adopted. It is now best known, of course, for the big and beautiful caverns twenty-seven miles to the southwest, the largest in America. They were first set apart as a national monument and then made a national park. Father's firm did some of the wiring when the park, open to visitors, was enlarged and modern elevators and more electric lights were added. You can now descend 750 feet to the main level as easily as going up or down by elevator in an office building. Thousands of people from all over the world do so every year. Thanks to tourists, a potash mine, and oil development in the area, the population of Carlsbad has doubled every decade since 1930.

Dad was a very strong man. He neither smoked nor drank. He had been a boxer at one time. To win a small bet, he once gave a dramatic demonstration of his strength by lifting the rear of a Ford truck and holding it off the ground long enough for a wheel with a flat tire to be changed. Robert and I inherited some of his strength. This has saved my neck several times in strange places. It helped Robert mine uranium at Grant, New Mexico, and molybdenum at Climax, Colorado, and later to operate successfully two Leadville bars and grills patronized by some of the most virile local residents.

I was born in Carlsbad on November 1, 1940. Life at the Happy Valley farm became unhappy within the space of a few months while I was still a small boy. My parents were divorced and both remarried, my father soon and my mother later. Dad then developed a rare form of cancer involving the nervous system. His big strong body slowly wasted away. All that we owned went for treatments, and everything was tried. There were trips to specialists and X-ray and radium therapy. Nothing worked. After dwindling from more than two hundred pounds to ninety pounds, he died and was buried in Carlsbad. He was only thirty-six years old.

My brother and I—he was twelve and I was seven at the time—then began a wandering life with our mother as she moved from job to job. She had few skills but plenty of courage and determination. She managed restaurants and bars and at times games in gambling casinos. The last are entirely legal in Nevada and many other parts of the West. Their operators demand of employees the same probity, sobriety, and expertise that bankers require of their tellers and cashiers.

We lived for at least short periods in Ruidoso, Hobbs, Santa Fe, and Las Vegas, New Mexico; in El Paso, Midland, and Lubbock, Texas; in Phoenix and Tucson, Arizona; in Los Angeles and San Francisco; and finally in Denver and Leadville, Colorado. Our mountain troops trained near Leadville in World War II. There wasn't much time to make friends, and one year I went to seven or eight different schools in almost as many cities.

There were no luxuries, but we didn't miss any meals, and there was some fun. We had a good summer in Mora, New Mexico, at a logging camp in which Jesse Midland, my Texan stepfather, had an interest. The air was clear and cool. When we first went up, we had to cut pine boughs, put them on the floor, and throw a blanket over them for beds. I was only eleven or twelve but grabbed an ax and did my share of chopping and trimming trees for the sawmill. I never felt better. Whether you burn it, sleep on it, or just look at it, there is something special about a tree that you cut yourself.

We also managed to make or listen to a lot of music, mostly Western and Mexican, on the radio, record player, and jukebox. The cowboys now drive automobiles, some of them even fly light airplanes, but they still sing about horses and campfires. As a boy, I had a flute, a harmonica, drums, and finally a guitar. I had no formal instruction with these instruments but learned to make noise with each of them.

I have a vivid memory of Mexicans singing in the night "Cielito Lindo" ("Beautiful Sky"), with its rousing chorus of "Ay! ay! ay! ay!" and of hearing "La Golondrina," "Adelita," "La Rancherita," and "La Cucaracha," the last a *corrido* commemorating a cockroach and commenting on the charms of girls in El Paso, Chihuahua City, and elsewhere. It was the marching song of Pancho Villa's revolutionary army and has outlived him by many years. There were songs like "Deep in the Heart of Texas" and "The Yellow Rose of Texas," which is not about a flower but about a girl. It was written originally about a slave beauty named Emily. General Antonio López de Santa Anna of Mexico dallied with her in his silken tent when he should have been getting ready for the Battle of San Jacinto. If you go to school very long in Texas, you soon hear about Santa Anna if not about Emily.

There also were ballads like "Casey Jones," "Home on the Range," "Poor Lonesome Cowboy," and "Oh, Bury Me Not on the Lone Prairie." Just before I enlisted, some of Leadville's history was used as the basis of an American opera, *The Ballad of Baby Doe*. It is based on the incredible story of Horace Austin Warner Tabor, who made and lost huge fortunes in silver mining, and his beautiful second wife, Elizabeth McCourt, better known as Baby Doe. Called "Silver Dollar" Tabor, he was mayor of Leadville, lieutenant governor, and briefly a United States senator. Before he died, he told Baby Doe to hold on to his last property, the Matchless Mine. She lived beside it in poverty for years and, half-starved, finally froze to death. Tabor gave Leadville an opera house that still stands. It has been restored in recent years.

As a boy, I had guns and dogs—chows, cocker spaniels, and shepherds. We always had animals around and seemed to like them better than people. My brother says the first gun I fired was a shotgun. When I was nine or ten, I was shooting rabbits and trying for bobcats in the cliffs around Carlsbad. I shot grouse on the wing with a .22-caliber pistol. In fact, I was a better shot with a pistol at fifty yards than most men are with a rifle. When I was twelve or thirteen, I often made a pack roll out of a couple of blankets, took along some food and a pistol, and spent a week or two by myself roaming and hunting in the mountains.

One day as I was walking near the Tabor Grand Opera House on Main Street in Leadville, I noticed some boxers sparring. They were training for a Golden Gloves tournament. A man invited me to try out and put me into some white trunks. He matched me with a boy who was fast on his feet and had boxed a little. He beat a regular *tap-tap-tap* on my head but simply didn't hurt me. I had trouble hitting him, but every time I did, I knocked him through the ropes. After three rounds, my white trunks were covered with his blood, and I was the winner. I was offered another match but didn't see any point in running the risk of getting my head bashed in just for sport.

Still, I began to get into more and more fights. Somebody would say something that I thought reflected on my family, and before I knew it I'd be hitting him. I couldn't pick unimportant people. I'd always have to tangle with the son of the head of the Chamber of Commerce or the brother of the Mayor, people like that, and I was soon very unpopular with the big people in town and known as a "rotten" kid.

I quit school after the tenth grade and went hitchhiking across the country. I took a look at everything and a close look at myself. I was a dropout. I had no trade. When I returned to Leadville, I decided to enlist. I felt the Air Force could do things for me.

I thought of all this as my head began to clear on that June morning at Lackland. My musing was interrupted by a barking voice of authority.

"Let's go, let's go!" somebody commanded. "You're not home, you're at Lackland! Everybody up and at 'em!"

I fell out of the bunk and stumbled to a mess hall. After a big breakfast, I began to discover what the Air Force could do for me—and what I could do for the Air Force.

Honor, Duty, and Radar

3 I WAS ONE of nearly a hundred recruits, mostly Southerners, for whom Lackland was the "gateway to the Air Force" that week. We had a lot of soft-spoken boys from Alabama, Georgia, and Mississippi. Some had been all over, some were away from home for the first time. American airmen eventually go to the ends of the earth, but nearly all of them go to Lackland first.

"3700th PERSONNEL PROCESSING CENTER," read a sign on the structure to which we reported, but the place was known locally as the Green Monster. It was green and it was big, but it was only a small part of Lackland, which spreads over three thousand acres and usually is populated by twenty thousand servicemen and fifteen hundred civilians. It has schools for chaplains, officers, the Women in the Air Force, and sentry dogs, besides being the largest basic-training center for new airmen. But big as it is, Lackland is just one of seven huge bases in and around San Antonio. Together they give the 250-year-old city the biggest and most varied permanent military establishment of the United States government.

Training soldiers, especially airmen, is the biggest local industry and has been for some time. On the whole, those responsible do a good job. They imbue young men with the ideals of "honor, duty, and country" while shaping them physically into fighting men and at least beginning their education in the electronic and engineering complexities of the newest tools of war. A lot of gadgets that were new as recently as World War II are now out of date. This is especially true in the Air Force. But there has been little change in some of the things that happen to new soldiers during their first few days of service.

Those of us who came from Colorado had been given tests and physical examinations at Leadville and Denver. That was just the beginning. Doctors and dentists checked us over at Lackland; some new soldiers got their teeth fixed for free. Our blood was typed. We were fingerprinted. We were immunized against tetanus, smallpox, typhoid fever, and other diseases. To my surprise, this was done not with needles but with air-gun injectors that looked like something out of a James Bond movie. No pain, just a wetness on the arm.

We were given fast and very close haircuts. There was supposed to be a choice of crew cut, flattop, or white sidewall. A few heads actually were shaved. Somebody asked why, and the answer was, "You might have lice."

"Who me?" demanded several indignantly.

"Sure, you," retorted a sergeant. "They're not as common as they used to be, but anybody can pick 'em up. Even Napoleon had 'em. That's why he always kept his hand stuck in his coat. He was scratching himself."

We were shown how to make a "military bed" with "hospital corners." We were given dog tags. We were issued clothing. This took the better part of a day. Experts started with tape measures and worked on us from the skin out. Besides an outfit to wear, we were given a big green barracks bag full of things. While you have a serial number from the time you enlist and nearly everything is "by the numbers" in the service, you have your name on your clothing. Besides helping the laundry keep things straight, this is supposed to boost morale. I did feel a little proud when I saw "SADLER" in block letters on my blouse, even if it didn't fit as well as it could. The name tags are also a blessing for people like me who can't remember names. You don't have to guess a soldier's name if you can read it off his tape. When I enlisted, most name tags were black lettering on white tape or gold lettering on a black tape. Later in Vietnam, both were changed to black lettering on an olive-drab background.

Even before we had all our clothes, we began to be "briefed" and "oriented" by lectures, motion pictures, and booklets as to what our duties and privileges were. The latter are substantial. If they were better known, I think military careers would be more popular and draft-card burnings fewer. If you are in the armed services, you don't need to worry about the necessities of life—food, clothing, and shelter. They are free, and you can spend your pay to buy the luxuries, like cigarettes and beer, at discounts at the post exchange. The post exchange, incidentally, is America's third largest retailer, ranking behind only Sears Roebuck and the A&P.

If you want more education, the service can be your high school and even your college. In addition to teaching war tasks, the military operates a multimillion-dollar General Educational Development program. This involves correspondence courses, in which about a million servicemen enroll each year, on-base classrooms, and partly or wholly paid tuition in civilian schools and colleges. Nobody makes you take them, but the courses are available if you want them. I heard that a chief warrant officer at Fort Devens, Massachusetts, who had been a high-school dropout, earned a Rutgers University degree. A total of 1,316 servicemen received degrees through the program in 1965. There are also pension and insurance benefits, and veterans are given preference by law in competitions for almost all civil-service jobs.

Then came basic training, partly "orientation" on Air Force customs, but mostly hard physical activity beginning at 5 A.M. and continuing until lights-out at 9 P.M. We learned the old-fashioned "hup-two-hip-foah" of close-order drill. It was pretty rugged. We ran a mile each morning, did calisthenics, negotiated obstacle courses, cleaned our barracks, stood inspection, mounted guard, drew KP.

The rigors of basic training are so well advertised and exaggerated that some soldiers develop diarrhea when they start it. But I had no problems—I liked the Air Force. Thanks to my mountain-developed marksmanship, I had the highest score on our first day at the rifle range. The hot July weather of San Antonio did not bother me, but a man or two keeled over from it nearly every day. Still, this heat was valuable conditioning for Vietnam and other places where the sun really blazes.

Soldiers feel history as well as heat in San Antonio. Feathered Indians, armored Spanish horsemen carrying clanking harquebuses, Santa Anna's Mexicans, troops of the Republic of Texas and the Confederacy, and our own soldiers and airmen have trained and sometimes fought over this sunbaked area. Ulysses S. Grant, Robert E. Lee, Philip Sheridan, and many other generals since their time have served in San Antonio. Many longtime soldiers like the place so much that they retire there.

The Alamo, the chapel of a Spanish mission dating from 1718, is the most famous of the local historical sites that keep alive the memory of old battles. It was in the news again in 1958 because of *13 Days to Glory*, a book about the battle there, written by Lon Tinkle, a Dallas newspaperman. With a dozen other trainees, I took a bus ten miles into San Antonio and visited the Alamo on the first day I had a pass during basic training. Partly original construction and partly restored, it stands on a plaza near the post office. An eloquent line carved in a monument outside summarizes the heroic story for the visitor in these words: "Thermopylae had its messenger of defeat. The Alamo had none."

Thermopylae is a pass in Greece. There, in 480 B.C., King Leonidas and three hundred Spartans confronted the whole invading Persian army of Xerxes. The pass was only fourteen yards wide, and the Spartans were brave, tough professional soldiers. In savage fighting, they stopped the Persians for three days and nights, piling up mountains of dead, until a local traitor showed the invaders a flanking mountain path that enabled them to attack Leonidas and his men from the rear. He and nearly all his men fought until killed, but at least one escaped with the news.

Soon after the Texas Revolution began, some one hundred and fifty Texans were surrounded inside the Alamo by an army of several thousand under General Antonio López de Santa Anna, the Mexican dictator. The Texans included such notable frontiersmen as James Bowie and Davy Crockett and were commanded by William Barrett Travis, a twenty-seven-year-old lieutenant colonel from South Carolina and Alabama. As the enemy encircled the Texans, Travis sent off, on February 24, 1836, a moving letter, a facsimile of which is displayed today in the Alamo.

"To the People of Texas and all Americans in the world," he wrote. "I am besieged by a thousand or more of the Mexicans under Santa Anna. I have sustained a continual bombardment and cannonade for 24 hours & have not lost a man. The enemy has demanded a surrender at discretion, otherwise the garrison are to be put to the sword if the fort is taken—I have answered the demand with a cannon shot, and our flag still waves proudly from the walls—*I shall never surrender or retreat.*

"Then, I call on you in the name of Liberty, of patriotism & everything dear to the American character, to come to our aid with all dispatch—The enemy is receiving reinforcement daily & will no doubt increase to three or four thousand in four or five days. If this call is neglected, I am determined to sustain myself as long as possible & die like a soldier who never forgets what is due to his own honor & that of his country—VICTORY OR DEATH."

A band of thirty-two men from the town of Gonzales heeded the plea and made their way through the lines and into the Alamo after midnight on the night of March 1–2. They were not enough. The besiegers stormed the mission on March 6, and all 187 Texans were killed. Shouting, "Remember the Alamo!" Texans under Sam Houston a few weeks later, on April 21, captured Santa Anna, destroyed his army, and won independence at San Jacinto.

Texans have built a shaft twenty-five feet taller than the Washington Monument commemorating this victory, and San Antonio celebrates the anniversary each year with a week-long fiesta. Fort Sam Houston on Government Hill, oldest of the local bases and headquarters of the Fourth Army, is named, of course, for the victor of San Jacinto.

Scorpio-born Theodore Roosevelt recruited and trained his Rough Riders in San Antonio. Douglas MacArthur attended the West Texas Military Academy, just across the street from Fort Sam Houston, and returned there later as a captain of engineers and then a general. In Fort Sam Houston's complex of two-story brick officers' residences, Number 617, B Section, bears a bronze plaque reading: "Occupied by 2nd Lieutenant & Mrs. Dwight D. Eisenhower, 1 July 1916."

Lieutenant Benjamin D. Foulois, who rose from private to major general, brought the Army's first airplane to Fort Sam Houston in 1910, and San Antonio added a new dimension as the center of military aviation. Lieutenant Thomas E. Selfridge, for whom Michigan's Selfridge Field is named, was killed earlier as a passenger in a crash with Orville Wright at Fort Myer, Virginia, but the first Army pilot to crash to his death did so at Fort Sam Houston. He was Lieutenant George Maurice Kelly, an English-born officer who had served in the Philippines and China. On May 10, 1911, to avoid hitting a tent filled with women and children in landing, he banked his Curtiss biplane too sharply and was killed. Kelly Air Force Base, adjoining Lackland, is named for him. Brooks Air Force Base, southeast of the city, is named for Cadet Sydney Johnson Brooks, Jr., a native of San Antonio and a former reporter on the San Antonio *Light*, who crashed to his death at Kelly Field on November 13, 1917. Randolph Air Force Base is named for Captain William M. Randolph, a Kelly Field flyer from Austin, who was killed in 1928 in a takeoff at Gorman, Texas.

Lackland, where at least a million airmen have had basic training, is named for Frank Dorwin Lackland, who began as a private in the District of Columbia National Guard and rose to brigadier general. As commandant of Kelly Field in the thirties, he saw the need and possibilities of a great training center. Reflecting a new and safer era of aviation, he lived to retirement and died in bed in 1943 at Walter Reed Hospital in Washington, D.C.

Before you complete basic training at Lackland, the Air Force by interviews and tests tries to find out which of its forty-four job fields interest you most and for which of them you are best qualified. These fields include intelligence, photomapping, weather, fire fighting, air traffic, guided-missile systems, atomic weapons, radio-radar systems, and armament-systems maintenance. These are just general areas; the actual jobs run into the hundreds. Most have little to do with piloting an airplane, something in which I was not especially interested, fortunately.

I put myself down for armament maintenance because of my interest in and success with guns. The interviewer thought this was logical too but explained that the immediate needs of the service as well as qualifications and wishes figure in advanced training assignments. I then took a lot of aptitude tests. These involved arithmetic reasoning, tool functions, figure recognition, pattern analysis, and so on. Together they were called the Airman Classification Battery. They were replaced the following year by the Airman Qualifying Examinations, which are believed to be a more accurate way of determining capabilities.

I think I made a reasonable showing on the tests, but instead of work on guns, I was chosen for radar training. Radar specialists were needed at the time. In July, with three weeks of basic training still to go, a score of us and all our gear were bundled into a bus. We rolled east over Highway 90, across Texas and Louisiana, to Keesler Air Force Base, just west of Biloxi, Mississippi, on the Gulf of Mexico.

Biloxi is an old city, halfway between New Orleans and Mobile, and is named for an Indian tribe. It gets just as hot as San Antonio but, because of the Gulf breezes, maybe not as often. Like Texas, it has been under six flags, including that of the forgotten West Florida Republic. Keesler is named for Lieutenant Samuel Reeves Keesler, an air hero of World War I, who was born in Greenwood, Mississippi. He was flying as an observer in France when his plane was attacked by four German Fokkers. Keesler shot down the leading one, but his pilot, Lieutenant Harold W. Riley, was hit, and their plane crashed.

"Keesler," Riley said later, "fired all the way down and after we crashed, although he had been shot three times through the chest and three times in the abdomen. The three Huns hung over us at low altitude and kept firing after we were clear of the wreck. Keesler was hit in the hip before we could get under cover. From 5:15 P.M. until midnight he received no medical attention, but showed wonderful self-control and won the admiration of German soldiers who came to look at him when we reached a dressing station." He died next day at a German field hospital in France. He received the Distinguished Service Cross posthumously for bravery in action, and the base at Biloxi was named for him in 1949. It is the home of the Technical Training Air Force Headquarters and has schools for training radio and radar operators and radar maintenance technicians, as well as several advanced courses in radar use.

While getting into this, we continued basic training and found it a bit more demanding than at Lackland. For one thing, there was a noncom known as Sergeant Mickey Mouse. He was about five feet five inches tall, wore Bermuda shorts and a pith helmet. He looked like a barrel on two broomsticks. Besides resembling Walt Disney's famous cartoon character, he epitomized the hard-boiled, slave-driving sergeant. While everything had been clean enough at Lackland, the floors at Keesler were polished until they were like glass. Field-grade officers sometimes took off their shoes when entering for fear of leaving marks.

Radar is interesting and important. A good case can be made for its doing more than any other single device in winning World War II for the United States and Great Britain. When I learned about this and saw radar equipment for the first time at Keesler, I gradually forgot some of my disappointment at not being assigned to guns as I had asked.

The average person knows nothing of the wonders of radar except that it may trap him as a speeder if he drives too fast in his automobile and sometimes figures in weather forecasts. It is based on a simple principle, but its application is infinitely complex, and its development has a long history. In accepting a medal back in 1922 from the Institute of Radio Engineers in New York, Guglielmo Marconi, the father of radio, reported noticing in his experiments that metallic objects sometimes miles away reflected and deflected radio waves.

"It seems to me," he continued, "that it should be possible to design apparatus by means of which a ship could radiate or project a divergent beam of these rays in any desired direction, which rays, if coming across a metallic object, such as another steamer or ship, would be reflected back to a receiver screened from the local transmitter on the sending ship, and thereby immediately reveal the presence and bearing of the other ship in fog or thick weather."

That same year, Dr. A. Hoyt Taylor and Leo C. Young of the Naval Research Laboratory noticed that communication from a radio station was interrupted when a small steamer moved in the path of the signals. This and Marconi's suggestion started a lot of systematic research. A transmitter and receiver were set up on opposite sides of the Potomac River, and passing boats interfered with the reception. In 1925, it was found that the surface of an intervening object acted as a mirror. By 1930, reflections from passing airplanes were detected, and by 1934 there were methods for measuring the distance of such planes.

The word "radar," the initials of "*r*adio *d*etecting *a*nd *r*anging," was coined in 1940 by a U.S. Navy officer. It spells the same forward and backward and is considered very appropriate for the device whose waves bounce back at the same speed at which they move forward.

Radar development meanwhile went forward in Great Britain. In 1935 a chain of five stations was built for the detection of hostile aircraft. In 1937 fifteen more were added, giving complete coverage along the east and south coasts from Scotland to the Isle of Wight. In the Battle of Britain (1940–1941), these stations detected approaching German bombers in time for the British fighters to get into the air, win that crucial struggle, and prevent invasion. The Germans also had their version of radar. Commando raids at Bruneval and other points on the French coast were staged to capture their equipment.

Every radarman soon hears the story of Joseph L. Lockard and George E. Elliott, Jr. Lockard, a Williamsport, Pennsylvania, boy, and Elliott, a Chicago youth, were privates in the 515th Signal Aircraft Service. On the morning of December 7, 1941, they were manning a mobile radar unit, equipment designated as SCR-270B, atop a bluff called Opana Point, on the north side of the island of Oahu, Hawaii. There also were mobile radar units nearby at Kawailoa and Kaaawa.

At 6:52 A.M., all three stations detected two approaching planes. These were reported, but the operators were told that the Navy had a reconnaissance flight out and that's what these planes were. All three stations were supposed to shut down at 7 A.M. Kawailoa and Kaaawa did so.

Elliott, however, was new at the work and eager for experience, and a truck that was supposed to take the two privates to breakfast failed to arrive, so they kept the Opana Point set working. At 7:02 A.M., Elliott noticed a bigger blip on the screen than he had ever seen and called Lockard. Thinking the equipment might be faulty, Lockard took over, only to confirm what Elliott had seen.

At 7:20 A.M., Lockard telephoned the radar-information center at Fort Shafter that he believed "a large flight of planes was approaching from about 130 miles out and slightly east of north of Oahu."

Unfortunately the lone officer on duty thought they were a flight of B-17's that he had heard were arriving from the United States.

"It's all right," he told Lockard.

The first planes had been Japanese reconnaissance

craft, and the "large flight," of course, were the Japanese bombers on the way to Pearl Harbor. They reached there at 7:55 A.M., thirty-five minutes after Lockard's call. If there had been action on his warning, many planes, ships, and lives might have been saved.

Lockard was promoted to sergeant, given the Distinguished Service Cross personally by Assistant Secretary of War Robert Patterson, and sent to the Signal Corps officers Candidate School at Fort Monmouth, New Jersey. He was a first lieutenant at the end of the war and returned to Williamsport and a job with the radio-tube division of Sylvania Electric Products Corporation. Elliott was promoted to sergeant and after the war moved to North Long Branch, New Jersey, and went to work for the New Jersey Bell Telephone Company in Asbury Park.

But old quarrels are forgotten with the passing of the years. Among the foreigners taking radar and other electronic courses at Keesler were several Japanese servicemen. After I learned to interpret a radar scope, read flight plans, draw aircraft movements and identify them, and something about minor radar maintenance, I looked at the bulletin board one day and discovered my name on a list of Air Force men ordered to Japan!

I had a twenty-day leave in Leadville, marked only by a couple of minor fights, and later climbed aboard a Flying Tiger C-121 outside San Francisco for the flight to the Far East. I was still seventeen.

Japan and Judo

4 AFTER SHORT refueling stops at Hawaii and Wake Island, our old bucket-seated Flying Tiger plane landed on Honshu, the main Japanese island, at the Tachikawa airfield, west of Tokyo. It was a foggy October night, and we took a bus over to Johnson Air Force Base at Irumagawa and checked into the transient barracks there at 4 A.M. American ground-combat troops had been withdrawn from Japan the previous February, but Air Force and Navy units continued there under a special security agreement signed with the peace treaty in 1951. This gave the United States the right to maintain armed forces in the country to secure Japan from attack.

The Aircraft Control and Warning Service, known jokingly as "all confused and wondering," to which I was assigned, was part of these forces. Johnson is another base named for a dead airman, in this case Lieutenant Colonel Gerald R. Johnson of the Fifth Air Force, who was killed in a 1945 accident. I waited there a week for orders, killing time drinking beer and chasing the pretty local girls. When my papers came, I was ordered to a radar station on Mount Mineokayama, near the town of Awa-Kamogawa on the Boso Peninsula across Tokyo Bay to the south. The station identified air traffic coming into the area, especially that from the south and east. It operated twenty-four hours a day.

I liked Japan from the start. It is a beautiful country that is not very cold in winter and is no hotter than Washington, D.C., in the summer. The people, at least the great majority of them, are polite and friendly to Americans.

Baseball is the leading sport. There are lots of cherry blossoms, kimono-garbed girls, and little bridges over small ponds full of fat fish. But the beauty is accompanied by hazards. There are also earthquakes, very frequent on some of the volcanic islands, and typhoons.

Small earthquakes occur about every other day. You are usually a little "seasick" the first time you see a hanging lamp begin to sway during a quake. Most of the tremors are harmless and you soon become used to them. Earthquakes are rated by a scale of numbers. To the Japanese, those that cause a slight movement of doors are of force 2. Those rattling windows are force 3. Those that shake houses are force 4. Tremors violent enough to break concrete walls are rated at force 5. The country town of Matushiro, 112 miles northwest of Tokyo, in a single day, November 22, 1965, had more than two thousand quakes, including three successive ones of force 4.

Typhoons are less frequent but more serious. A few days before I left, the biggest typhoon in twenty-four years swept much of the country, killing one thousand people and leaving four hundred thousand homeless. Tokyo had wind gusts of 160 miles an hour and sixteen to twenty inches of rain. American servicemen helped clear the wreckage and provide relief. The work was still going on when I arrived.

Tokyo claimed to be the biggest city in the world. Its more than ten million people made it bigger than New York and perhaps bigger than London. Air traffic in and out of the area is heavy. Our station was a busy one. There was nearly always something on our radar screens, but life at the station seemed dreamy luxury after the long work-jammed days of basic training.

Half the station staff were Japanese. They were soldiers of the Japanese Air Self-defense Force. They did half of the radar work and also helped teach the Americans enough of the Japanese language to understand and carry on an ordinary conversation. American money went a long way. Each barracks employed a Japanese houseboy. These houseboys, who were of all ages, kept the barracks clean, took care of boots and shoes, and were eager to supply anything you needed or wanted and at what they insisted were bargain prices.

There was leisure to read and study. Many did. I read my first science fiction and first Ian Fleming novels in Japan. There was time to fish and swim in Tokyo Bay, to visit the colorful villages in the neighborhood, to watch old and young Japanese fly kites and make wonderful things out of paper. When we had passes, we could take a train—and most Japanese trains are good, some of them the fastest in the world—around the bay past towns and temples to Tokyo.

I celebrated my eighteenth birthday, November 1, 1958, by exploring the attractions of Tokyo for the first time. A buddy went along. We had just been paid and, by Japanese standards, had a lot of money in our pockets. We took a train into the heart of the city and spent most of the day along the Ginza. This is both the Fifth Avenue and the Broadway of Tokyo. Traffic was frantic and on the left side of the street. We saw some of the usual tourist attractions and visited little and big shops, including the great department stores. One big store has a Buddhist altar on its roof. Others have fishing ponds, zoos, and observation platforms from which to view the city.

Polite girls at the doors bow and thank the customer for his business. Elevator operators bow at each stop and apologize for disturbing you. The most polite clerks in the world serve you. They sell television sets and the latest foreign records, traditional Japanese sashes and kimonos, and exotic oddities like chirping cicadas in small bamboo cages.

A customer can even order a wife or husband at Mitsukoshi, the largest department store in the Far East. It boasts a government marriage bureau. Men and women seeking mates leave their photographs, vital statistics, and a list of qualities they desire in a spouse. Marriage ceremonies are performed in a chapel in the store basement. For the equivalent of about $15, Mitsukoshi rents the bride a wedding dress, supplies a maid to dress her, and makes available an adjoining banquet hall where tea and cakes are furnished for guests.

Toward evening, my buddy and I found a bar. The Japanese are good brewers and distillers. In addition to their native wines, they have their own version of any drink made anywhere, including Scotch. Japanese beer is excellent—as good as German beer. We "bought" the bar, chased everybody out except some girls, and spent the night sampling everything. Next morning we had to borrow train fare back to the radar station from a GI we met on the street.

On a later visit, I noticed a tattoo artist at work on the Tokyo waterfront. I looked over his designs and had him put a small blue panther on my left arm. Long-haired scientists at the Office of Naval Research have worried about why soldiers and sailors get tattooed and whether there is anything crazy or abnormal about those who do. If a fellow has more than two tattoos, they say, he is likely to have some anxiety. Be that as it may, I agree that a fellow who has himself tattooed with his girl's name and then changes girls might well have something to worry about.

All sorts of people have had a small tattoo or two. Field Marshal Montgomery of Great Britain has a butterfly on his arm. The late King George V had a red-and-blue dragon that he got in Japan in the course of a voyage as a midshipman in the British Navy. King Frederik IX of Denmark had a lot of tattooing. Winston Churchill's American mother, Jennie Jerome, had a small one. A Metropolitan Opera singer named Rosalind Elias won a lot of newspaper notice in 1961 by going down to the Bowery in New York and having her name and social security number tattooed on her lower belly as a means of identification in the event of possible large-scale disaster.

An airman who had lived in Canada recalled seeing in the window of a Toronto tattoo artist a sign reading something like this: "Last Week! Be Prepared! Make It Easier to Identify Your Body After the Atom Blast. Let

Painless Pancho Do It for You Now While He Too Is Still Alive. Special Pre-Atomic Prices Now in Effect." I wasn't thinking about anything of the sort when I got my panther. I just had him done on the spur of the moment, with the vague idea that the experience would be interesting and that the panther might bring me luck.

I did have some luck. Within a few weeks, I was promoted to airman second class, which is equivalent to the Army's private first class. This put two stripes on my arm and raised my pay to more than $100 a month. I also won my high-school diploma by passing a General Educational Development test. This is an evaluation, and for military purposes the diploma the armed service issues is equivalent to a high-school diploma. Most schools also recognize it. I was promoted to tracking supervisor and given charge of a crew, half Japanese and half American.

I had luck off base too. I went skin diving, sometimes with Japanese friends, at every chance in the coves and inlets of Tokyo Bay. We sometimes actually caught and rode sand sharks. One day I felt a tug at my foot, looked down, and saw half a flipper gone and the dorsal fin of a shark cutting away. But I was unhurt. The Japanese, and many others, eat the meat of sharks and eels. They believe that eating eels strengthens their bodies to withstand heat. Mostly we dived amid the coral for the big moray and conger eels. When we found them, we'd go after them, usually successfully, with three-pronged spears. One day I speared one more than five feet long. When I reached down to grab him by the gills, his tail slapped across my face, broke my mask, and knocked it off. I had to let him go or suffocate, but again I was unhurt.

Another bit of luck was a Japanese girl friend named Yoko, a five-foot-two-inch living doll who worked at a bar downtown in Awa-Kamogawa. She was always glad to see me, but there was an Air Force policeman in the area who didn't like me. As soon as I'd get there, he would decide to declare the place off limits and come beating on the door. I'd escape by jumping fifteen feet out a back window into a muddy rice paddy. The filth on my boots made the barracks houseboy so mad that he kept urging me to find another girl. Each time I jumped, the hole in which I landed became a little deeper. I was knee-deep when I first jumped in the spring and waist-high by fall. But she was worth the trouble, and the policeman never caught me.

There was some violent anti-American sentiment in Japan at the time. This was before Edwin Reischauer, who had a Japanese wife, became our ambassador and improved relations. We would see pictures of agitators parading in newspapers and sometimes in the newsreels. The next year a scheduled visit of President Eisenhower to Japan was canceled for fear of violence. I never personally encountered any of this hostility. In fact, my experience was just the opposite.

One Japanese treated me like a son. His name was Aikawa Kaiichi. He was a man in his seventies who was a carpenter at the post and also a great judo and karate expert. He took me into his home and made me a member of his seaside village. This was Chikura, near Cape Nojima, to the southwest of our radar station. Thanks to Kaiichi's interest and friendship, I saw more of Japanese family life than do most Americans who go to Japan.

I am not much for religion, but because he invited me I even took part in the village religious festivals. These were colorful and noisy affairs. They get out the little temples, very old and of carved teakwood. Children get inside them and play gongs and flutes. Sometimes as many as fifteen children crowd into one of the little structures, which rest on poles. You and other men, maybe a hundred in all, then pick up the poles and hoist the temple and the children shoulder-high. You wear a sweatband around your head and a *happi* jacket with the village ideogram on the back. You go through the village, swinging back and forth and chanting, and carry the temple out to sea. As you weaken, the women come up and pour sake down your throat to keep your strength up. If a man gets drunk and falls down, as sometimes happens, another jumps in and takes his place.

The greatest thing Aikawa Kaiichi did for me was to teach me all he knew about judo and karate. These are second only to baseball in popularity in Japan. As the host nation, Japan added judo to the Olympic Games in 1964, and the Japanese team won the event. Kaiichi's body was proof of what these sports can do for a man. He had a tremendous amount of character in his face. It was very weathered and wrinkled, and his head was bald. But when he took off his shirt, you saw the firm, slim body of a twenty-year-old youth. He looked as if somebody had taken a chisel and carved his muscles out of marble. There was not an ounce of fat or flab.

Judo and karate are refinements of jiujitsu. Whole books have been written about them. Jiujitsu is the oldest and best-known system of unarmed self-defense. The idea is to conquer by yielding. The weight and strength of an opponent are used to pull or throw him off-balance and hurt or even kill him by pressures or blows to sensitive spots. A small man, or even a woman, expert at jiujitsu can rout a much bigger unskilled adversary. According to one legend, jiujitsu was first devised by the monks in ancient China to protect themselves from armed robbers. The Japanese adopted it first as a secret art restricted to the nobility. It later became a part of Japan's Army, Navy, and police training and was taught in schools.

"Jiujitsu" is written as two Japanese characters. The first means "gentle" or "to give way." The second means "art" or "practice." For "judo," the second syllable means "way" or "principle." The word was coined by the late Dr. Jigoro Kano, who in 1882 founded in Tokyo the Kodokan, literally a school for studying "the way." This involves ethics, moral training, and physical culture as well as winning hand-to-hand contests with maximum efficiency and minimum effort. From Tokyo, disciples of Dr. Kano took judo all over the world.

The judoka, or judo player, wears a simple uniform consisting of trousers, jacket, and belt. The color of the belt indicates your experience and rank. You start out with a white belt. If you defeat some experienced contestants, you advance to a brown belt; with some more wins, you come finally to the black belt. There are three grades of brown belts and several of the black. The judo hall, scene of matches and tournaments, is called the *dojo*. It is a place of culture and ceremony as well as of sweat and grunts.

Nobody is supposed to be killed or even seriously hurt in judo or karate. Matches are rough, utilizing some moves of boxing, wrestling, and even football, and opponents may yell and roar at each other, but they are ritualistic affairs governed by many rules. Points are won not by pinning an opponent to the mat, as in wrestling, but by maneuvering him into such a predicament that he must yield rather than risk broken bones, dislocated joints, or other serious injuries.

When a contestant is thus defeated, he usually says, *"Maitta!"* meaning, "I am beaten." Or he can signal this by tapping his adversary's jacket several times at the nearest spot. The winner must immediately relax his hold. If he does not, the referee will make him do so.

Judo is largely a matter of holds and throws. The newer karate emphasizes punches and kicks with the bare hands and feet. "Karate" literally means "empty hand." Both involve *atemiwaza*, the "art of attacking vital spots." These include the solar plexus and Adam's apple among others. Learning judo requires time and effort, but for most people it is easier than boxing or wrestling and probably more useful.

Aikawa Kaiichi began to give me judo lessons four hours a day, four or five days a week, either at his home or at the judo hut on the post. I tried to pay him, but except for a little cocoa for his child, he would accept nothing from me in return.

Soon after starting this, I bought a new judo suit with a white belt and wore it to the judo hut. Kaiichi happened to be ill that day and did not appear, but I found a little Japanese airman, a member of one of the radar crews, bowing and speaking to me. I had been in Japan long enough to know that when somebody bows to you, a response is required. I smiled and bowed to him.

What I didn't know was that he was offering me a fight. When I bowed back, I accepted his challenge. I am five feet nine inches tall and then weighed 165 pounds. He was only five feet four inches and weighed only 110 pounds, but he was a good black-belt judo man. He soon had my feet straight up in the air and my head three feet off the ground. I hit the wall—*boing!* It took him only twelve seconds to ruin me and discover that I knew nothing. They had to carry me back to the barracks.

"Here comes the expert!" somebody jeered. This did not discourage me. As I continued my judo with Kaiichi, my health and strength improved. My weight increased to around two hundred pounds, and I developed a seventeen-inch neck and seventeen-inch biceps. I lived and breathed judo day and night and went all out for it. I had a return match with the airman who bounced me off the wall, and this time I won.

I even mumbled about judo in my sleep, sometimes disturbing a Negro boy named Callinaw, who had the next bunk. Our radar station shared a mountain with harmless grass snakes and also some poisonous varieties. One night after an evening off post, I awoke to feel one snake crawling along my stomach and another going up the inside of my leg. If I yelled or moved, I was afraid they would bite me.

"Hey, Callinaw!" I whispered. "Callinaw."

"Yeah, yeah," he mumbled, "what ya want?"

"Callinaw, I got snakes in bed with me."

"Yeah, you been drinking that wine again."

"Aw, c'mon, Callinaw," I begged. "They're gonna bite me."

"Oh, leave me alone," he answered. "Let me go to sleep."

The fellows let me suffer for fifteen minutes and almost go out of my mind. Then I heard one of them laugh and say, "Grass snakes." I was so mad that I jumped out of the bunk, picked up a loaded footlocker weighing around sixty pounds, and hurled it through the door at the other end of the room.

I guessed accurately that Charles Pekala, a red-haired Polish-American boy, was responsible. Next morning I noticed him stripped naked and soaping himself in a warm shower. I grabbed a carbon dioxide fire extinguisher and turned its icy liquid on him in the hot shower, practically freezing him where it hit.

"Cut it out, Sadler!" he screamed. "Can't you take a joke?"

"Yes, yes," I agreed, "I'm laughing."

I continued to study judo with Aikawa Kaiichi and to work out with the toughest professionals in the neighborhood. In fact, during training, I never fought an amateur. I cut out drinking almost entirely. Drinking and judo don't mix, and moderation in all things is part of "the way." I felt better and looked better.

After eight months, Kaiichi and I agreed that I was ready for a major judo tournament. As I hadn't been in one before, he had to get special permission for me to enter. He did this one afternoon a few weeks before my nineteenth birthday. We went to the *dojo* at Takeyama. It was a busy place with white-costumed judo players of all belts practicing and fighting all over the building.

At 1 P.M., they called my name and the name of an opponent. He was a white-belted young fellow of about my weight and experience. We bowed to each other, and a referee said, "*Hajima mari*"—"Begin," and we went at it. I was strong and well trained, and after only a few minutes he tapped my jacket and gave up.

He no sooner walked off than they threw another man at me. He was tougher and took longer, but I beat him too and was still feeling eager and full of beans. Aikawa Kaiichi was happy and hugged me as if I were his son. They then tossed some fellows with brown belts and then black belts at me. I won nine straight fights that afternoon and began a tenth.

This man was big, fast, and smart. I'd get what I thought was a winning hold on him, but he would break it. He didn't have any better luck with me. By 7 P.M., it was beginning to get dark and other fighters were scheduled for the hall, so the referee decided to call it a draw. We bowed and shook hands all around. Aikawa Kaiichi was beside himself with joy.

In one afternoon, I had jumped six grades in the strict judo ranking to win my black belt. No other American, as far as anybody there knew, had ever advanced so far so fast. It takes most men at least a year, with several intermediate stops, to make black belt. It was the proudest and happiest day of my life at that time.

"Silver Wings upon Their Chests"

5 MY YEAR IN JAPAN went so fast that I wrote only half a dozen or so letters home. Before I realized it, I was back in the United States watching for right- instead of left-handed traffic when I crossed streets and having to do some of the things that had been done by houseboys in Japan. I was assigned to the 774th Aircraft Control and Warning Squadron at a radar site near Madera, California, that then had the code name of Shady Lady. It was part of the continental defense system. Our screens would pick up planes hundreds of miles away. In a matter of seconds they would be tracked, located, and identified. Fortunately all proved friendly craft.

From there I was sent to the Richards-Gebaur Air Force Base, south of Kansas City, Missouri, to study a new SAGE radar system. The initials stood for Semi-Automatic Ground Environment system radar, and I was a member of the first group to be taught its use. Radar is constantly being improved and its applications expanded. As this is written, I notice that Army scientists are using airborne radar to measure the thickness of the polar ice caps.

I was next assigned to Beale Air Force Base, forty miles north of Sacramento and eleven miles east of Marysville, California. It was formerly Camp Beale and is named for Edward F. Beale, a California pioneer who lived in the neighborhood. During World War II, German prisoners of war, many of them tough soldiers who served under Rommel in North Africa, were confined at Beale under maximum security.

Some of these men, lonely and thousands of miles

from home, made paint out of crushed chalk, matches, and ashes and sketched pictures on the thick concrete walls around them. Fifteen years later these could still be seen. Several were really beautiful. Sketches of some girls and a blind violinist I thought particularly attractive. Seeing this art by forgotten and unknown enemy soldiers caused me to become interested in sketching. I added it to my guitar playing and judo hobbies, but the last continued to be my overwhelming off-duty interest.

Radar work involves night and odd-hour assignments, but you are excused from a lot of routine and have considerable spare time to use as you like. While serving as crew chief and winning promotion to airman first class, I also taught judo to the 15th Air Force team and the local sheriff's department. I was doing all this as my four-year enlistment came to an end. I could have collected a bonus by reenlisting, but I was a little tired of radar. It gives you no chance to use judo, for one thing. Also, I hate cold weather, and there was a strong rumor than that I was about to be sent to the DEW (Distant Early Warning) line in the Arctic.

I became a civilian when my enlistment was up in June, 1962, and looked for a job back home in Colorado. Nobody was advertising for a twenty-one-year-old radar expert interested in judo. The stock market had just taken its biggest drop since 1929. There was trouble in the steel industry and some others. There were few jobs of any kind.

So a friend of mine named Walter Lane tossed my guitar and his drums into a 1953 Chevrolet, and we hit the road in an effort to make a living playing in bars, honky-tonks, shopping centers, and any place else that would have us. We earned $6 our first night. We added a Negro piano player and operated as a three-piece combination. I knew him only as Elmo. He lived around Marysville and was a fantastic musician. This guy taught me three chords, A, E, and B-7, and he said, "Everytime I nod my head, you change chords and play as fast as you can." We turned the volume up, and nobody every knew the difference. I did my first singing in public at this time and had so much trouble with "What Kind of Fool Am I?" and other hits of that year that I began to think about writing song lyrics myself.

We drove from Colorado through Wyoming, Montana, Washington State, Oregon, and back down into California. To make out, Lane and I got day jobs loading crates of fruit into boxcars for $1.10 an hour. The two of us were fast and strong enough to load a boxcar in a couple of hours. We would then play at night. It was backbreaking, and by August I was tired of it. I was getting nowhere.

I decided to reenlist for three years and this time to give the Army a whirl. I talked to a recruiting officer in Marysville and volunteered for the airborne paratrooper service. I saw this as a chance to use my judo training and to escape from radar work, which would have been my assignment if I had returned to the Air Force. Two days later I was shipped to Fort Ord, California, as a private first class because of my previous service.

I arrived there with just $3 in my pocket, the clothes on my back, and a little carry bag in which I had one pair of Levi's and a shirt. Many others, some volunteers and some draftees, reported there at the same time.

"Who's prior service here?" somebody asked. I was the only one who admitted any.

"All right," the fellow said, "we got a barracks over here. There are ninety-eight men in it. This is your barracks. Take these recruits and straighten 'em up."

I went into the barracks and found some of the wildest-looking monsters I'd ever seen, great hulking apes. I had never worked with people like this before. I didn't know what docks and warves the Army had scraped them off of. I went from floor to floor and on each selected two or three of the biggest, meanest-, baddest-looking numbers.

"You know what you are?" I asked them.

"What?" they said.

"You are a squad leader, that's what you are," I told them. "I want you to take this section and straighten them up." I made all the bad ones bosses—it worked.

Because of my prior service, I wasn't required to take basic training, but I volunteered for it. I wanted to learn soldiering from the grass roots. This isn't done very often, but some men like basic training and excel at it. In 1966, I read about Donald Brady, a nineteen-year-old boy from Oak Lawn, Illinois, running the mile in combat boots and fatigues in four minutes and forty-seven seconds in basic training at Fort Bliss, Texas.

I was in basic at Fort Ord when the crisis developed

over the Russian missiles discovered in Cuba. This inspired me to a small joke. I dictated an authoritative-sounding announcement into a tiny tape recorder and then played it in the recruit barracks.

"Your attention please, your attention please!" said my tape. "Please do not be alarmed. We have a message coming. All military personnel will report to their installations. All leaves and passes are canceled until further notice. Stay tuned to your Conelrad station." I ran this off on the little portable machine and told them it was coming over the air every five minutes. They began to run around frantically, some packing gear and some writing letters home. Looking back, it may not have been so funny.

Some Eskimo National Guardsmen from Alaska were at Fort Ord for training at the time. Some knew little English, and nobody knew what to do with them when they were off duty. A fellow finally took them fishing in Monterey Bay. This made them happy, and they caught a lot of fish. But the fish stank up the post when hung up to dry and had to be taken away. This made some of the Eskimos mad. When an Eskimo gets mad, he swells up and sputters.

I had a good time at Fort Ord and, as one of the top men in the class, was selected to attend a three-week advanced leadership course between basic and advanced individual training. I ranked second in that course. I then went into advanced individual training, which was infantry and light weapons, and had no trouble qualifying for airborne training.

For this I was sent to the Army Infantry School at Fort Benning, Georgia. It was cold when I arrived there a few days before Christmas in 1962. There was nothing to do for several days, and I spent some of the time looking at the paintings and insignia exhibits on the history of parachutes and airborne warfare around the post. They are impressive and cover all nations.

General Billy Mitchell, according to official Fort Benning history, conceived the idea of parachuting troops into battle. He wanted to "climb over" the western front in World War I and soon afterward demonstrated the idea at Kelly Field in San Antonio. Six soldiers parachuted from a Martin bomber, assembled their weapons, and were ready for action in less than three minutes. But our military paid no attention, and Soviet Russia and Nazi Germany were the first to have and use big paratrooper units. The Germans won quick victories with them in Poland, Norway, Holland, and Crete.

Paratrooper training began at Fort Benning in 1940, and the records of our World War II airborne divisions are as glorious as any in the annals of warfare. These included the 11th in the Pacific and the 13th, 17th, 82nd, and 101st in Europe. The soldiers who held Bastogne in the Battle of the Bulge and Brigidar General Anthony C. McAuliffe, who said "nuts" to the demand to surrender, were men of the 101st Airborne (Screaming Eagle) Division. Traditions of these famous units inspire fledgling paratroopers.

My paratrooper training began in freezing weather

right after New Year's Day of 1963. It was rugged. We fell in at about 4:30 A.M. Then we would go to breakfast and in not much more than ten minutes had to eat, get out, and resume formation. We would run a quarter- or half-mile to a training area and then, stripped to the waist, would run some more. When we stopped, a cloud of steam would rise from the group in the cold winter air.

First came the physical training and a physical-fitness test. If a student failed this, he got no further and was sent back to his previous or some other ground unit. Six properly executed pull-ups on a bar over your head were required. Kicking, "bicycling," or jerking motions with the body or legs were not acceptable. A student had to perform at least twenty-two properly executed push-ups and a minimum of twenty sit-ups. I did so many push-ups, I think I pushed the state of Georgia six inches away from the rest of the country. As an endurance test, the student had to run a mile in eight and a half minutes or less—in his boots. He had to perform eighty knee bends in two minutes. Bending your knees only and keeping your body erect, you drop until you can touch the ground with your fingertips and then again stand erect. Because your knees bend when you hit the ground properly in jumps, paratroopers refer scornfully to all earthbound soldiers as "straight legs."

Ground-training week came next. You were shown how to fall properly, distributing the shock over your body so as to minimize the chance of injury. You jump out of the mock door of an airplane and are confronted with a lot of simulated danger situations to keep you mentally alert. Physical training continues.

Then came tower-training week. Jumps in harness from a little 34-foot tower taught us how to control our bodies until the parachute opened and also helped in overcoming the natural fear of height. We were taught how to manipulate and control the parachute during descent and given instruction in emergency landing. We then advanced to three big 250-foot towers. These were originally built for the 1939-1940 New York World's Fair and were later in Hightstown, New Jersey, before being moved to Fort Benning. They are tall enough to simulate real jump conditions. At the Fair, lines guided the parachutes to the ground; but at Fort Benning, you jump free just as from an airplane. The wind blew one fellow in my group two blocks, and he landed on the roof of the Officers Training School Barracks.

The training is good. They get you so programmed, so used to responding to commands, that you automatically do whatever they tell you to do. You don't think about it. You just react and do it. At this point, you are ready for the real thing.

Your first parachute jump from an airplane is one of life's great experiences. Mine came on my sixth or seventh flight. For some boys it comes on their first time in an airplane. You wait in line before the door. You hear the engines and the wind roaring.

"Stand up, hook up," orders the jumpmaster. "Check your static line, check your equipment."

I shuffled to the door asking myself, Am I going to jump?

"Let go," came the command.

I was still asking myself that question when I went out the door. There was the roar of the engines just ahead. The wind hit me like the blow of a typhoon. It heaved me back, and I could feel my body swing around. Then the parachute opened with a jerk.

Then suddenly all was quiet. I was floating down and could hear nothing. Then I began to laugh, and I heard others in the air around me laughing too. We were all so happy that our chutes had opened and we were alive that we were laughing our fool heads off.

"Quiet up there," ordered an instructor as I came down. "Quiet up there. Straighten up."

Very elated, I hit the ground with properly bent knees, rolled up the parachute, and doubled-timed with it off the muddy field.

During the last week of training, you are required to make five jumps, two of them with full field equipment. When you finish these, the officers and instructors who have been driving you hard for weeks suddenly congratulate you, and you are given your parachutist's badge with ceremony. Your pay also jumps $55 a month and stays there as long as you make at least one jump every three months.

They really run you ragged in jump school. It is something every soldier should do once but never twice. At Fort Benning, the parachutist's badge is called the "badge of courage" with good reason.

It is a silver representation of a dropping parachute with feathered wings on each side. The senior parachutist's badge has a star at the top of the parachute. To earn this, you must participate in at least thirty jumps, fifteen with combat equipment, including two night jumps, one as jumpmaster. In addition, you must graduate from a jumpmaster school or have been a jumpmaster in combat.

A master parachutist's badge has a wreath around the star. Among other things, this requires sixty-five jumps, twenty-five with combat equipment, four night jumps, and five mass tactical jumps that culminate an air-assault problem.

I was happy to have the plain silver wings. Receiving them gave me my happiest day since winning the black belt in Japan. I began to think about writing a song involving the airborne. I had no idea what it would be, but I wanted it to include the line "silver wings upon their chests."

"Men of the Green Beret"

6 I HAD READ a recruiting booklet about the Army's Special Forces, and as soon as I had my silver wings I volunteered. I reported for training at what is now the John F. Kennedy Center for Special Warfare at Fort Bragg, North Carolina. Bragg was originally an artillery range. It is a huge place, some two hundred square miles—three times the area of the District of Columbia—much of it still a pine forest.

Besides having the J.F.K. Center for Special Warfare on Smoke Bomb Hill, Bragg is headquarters for the XVIII Airborne Corps. This includes the 82nd at Bragg and the 101st Airborne Division at Fort Campbell. Some of my jump-school classmates joined these famous units. Included in the Special Forces operation is what used to be called the Psychological Warfare School, offering instruction in many subjects that have come along in fighting since General Braxton Bragg, whose name the place bears, commanded the Confederates and was defeated nearby in the last North Carolina battle of the Civil War.

The Special Forces were being beefed up. They were formed at Bragg in 1952, when psychological-warfare training was moved there from Fort Riley, Kansas, where it had been formally started two years earlier. They began to wear green berets, but somebody banned them, and the Special Forces units were kept small. Any new outfit anywhere has to earn acceptance. Special uniforms and insignia may be resented by those who don't wear them and don't know the reasons for them. There's a lot to be said for the old and orderly way of doing things.

Actually, special warfare is ancient stuff. Stained-glass windows in the new Special Warfare Memorial Chapel at Fort Bragg trace it back to Gideon's victory over a superior force of Midianites in 1245 B.C. Gideon had each of his three hundred men light a lamp and blow a trumpet. Thinking they were outnumbered, the Midianites fled in panic.

The history of Special Forces dates back to 1755 and the French and Indian War, when Rogers' Rangers were formed from the New Hampshire Militia to conduct "unconventional warfare" against the Indians. This type of warfare helped defeat the British during the Revolution. For example, Francis Marion, South Carolina's Swamp Fox, cut British supply and communication lines.

More direct unit lineage dates to organization of the First Special Service Forces, formed in 1942 at Fort William Henry Harrison, Montana. This was a joint United States–Canadian force commanded by Major General Robert T. Frederick. It made the initial assault on Kiska Island in the Aleutians in 1943 to combat the Japanese occupation and subsequently saw action in Italy and France. The crossed arrows and distinctive unit insignia of present-day Special Forces were first authorized for wear by the First Special Service Forces.

Unconventional warfare during World War II took on another form with the Office of Strategic Service (OSS), under command of Colonel William L. Donovan. Teams consisting of two officers and a radio operator were parachuted into France. Later, operational groups consisting of two officers and thirteen men were deployed in France.

One OSS detachment saw action in northern India and Burma. Also operating in this theater was another special-warfare unit: Brigadier General Frank Merrill's 5307th Composite Unit, better known as Merrill's Marauders. This three-thousand-man force fought five major and seventeen minor battles with the Japanese in Burma.

Additional lineage and tradition stem from the Ranger battalions. The 1st Ranger Battalion was formed in 1942 at Carrickfergus, Northern Ireland, under command of Colonel William O. Darby. The unit was later employed in the Tunisian, Sicilian, and Italian campaigns. Later the Rangers spearheaded the Anzio invasion, and two of their battalions were wiped out. On D-Day, Ranger battalions assaulted the cliffs of Pointe du Hoe. A Ranger battalion spearheaded the invasion of Leyte Gulf and the island of Luzon. Darby's Rangers were disbanded in 1944, and Colonel Darby was killed in action in Italy in 1945.

The Rangers were briefly reactivated in 1948 in the Canal Zone. They were activated again in 1950 at Fort Benning as eight Ranger companies. Seven were used as long-range patrols and spearheads for attacks and specialized missions in Korea. The companies were deactivated in less than a year, after suffering more than fifty percent casualties. The present Special Forces formally came into being on June 20, 1952, at Fort Bragg. Colonel Aaron Bank was the first commander.

President John F. Kennedy gave the Special Forces a great boost. Because of the success of Fidel Castro in Cuba and other troublemakers elsewhere, President Kennedy became deeply interested in guerrilla and counterguerrilla warfare. He visited Bragg in 1961 and liked what he saw. He ordered a big increase in the Special Forces and restored the green beret. He urged the troopers to wear it "proudly" and predicted that "it will be a mark of distinction and a badge of courage in the difficult days ahead." The letter that he wrote them is displayed at the Special Forces Warfare Center Museum. There was no lowering of standards. Everybody still had to be a paratrooper to start and had to undergo additional difficult training.

Wearers of green berets continued to be few and little known to the public. Even in Fayetteville, North Carolina, adjoining Fort Bragg, a Green Beret buying gasoline was mistaken for a foreign soldier. "It's nice you speak such good English," said the filling-station attendant.

His mistake was natural. Soldiers from fifty nations, including England, France, Japan, the Philippines, Taiwan, Canada, West Germany, nearly every Latin-American country, and Australia, have trained at Bragg in recent years. Many had berets. The beret is a foreign cap. The Bancroft Cap Company of Framingham, Massachusetts, which made the official berets for the Special Forces, had to import the rough material from the Basque country of France because the knitting equipment required did not exist in America. Foreign soldiers like Field Marshal Montgomery and the British and Canadian commandos have worn berets for years. The tank crews and seamen of many nations think them both jaunty and practical.

While the Special Forces are nothing like the French Foreign Legion, except in remote and rugged assignments, they also include some foreigners. This is also true of other Army units, the Navy, Air Force, and Marines. One of the first prisoners to escape from the Communists in Laos was German-born Dieter Dengler, a Navy lieutenant and a naturalized citizen. Most of the foreigners in Special Forces were career soldiers who had immigrated to America. We had some men who had fought with the British in Malaya, some Czechs, some West Germans, a lot of different nationalities. One of my friends was from the Philippines.

The big idea of Special Forces is to train men and units capable of parachuting and, in the words of a Bragg booklet, "infiltrating deep into enemy-controlled territory, there to contact local dissidents and organize, train, equip, and advise them as guerrillas to work against the common enemy." Of the many qualifications required. the ability to teach others is the most important. Each twelve-man Special Forces "A" team is supposed to be able to instruct fifteen hundred guerrillas.

Special Forces "A" teams, the operational and fighting units, are composed of a commanding officer, (usually a captain), and executive officer, (a first lieutenant), a sergeant in charge of operations, and nine specialists, (also usually senior sergeants). The latter include an intelligence sergeant, medical and assistant medical specialists, heavy- and light-weapons leaders, two radio experts, and two engineer specialists, who are called demo men.

With a few suggestions from others, I later wrote and sang a song called "The 'A' Team," after being a member of several of them. These are the lines:

> Twelve men strong and true,
> Twelve men fight for you,
> On their heads a beret of green,
> Twelve men invincible,
> The "A" team.
>
> Twelve men heard the call,
> Ready to give their all,
> They bring hope where they are seen,
> Twelve men invincible,
> The "A" team.
>
> From Asia's tropical jungle rains
> All the way to Africa's burning plains,
> Wherever there's trouble night or day,
> Go the men of the Green Beret
> To fan the fire of freedom's dream,
> The "A" team.*
> Twelve men invincible,

Every "A" team member is cross-trained in at least two specialties besides his own, making it possible for the team to split into smaller detachments and also to get a message out if both radiomen are disabled. It is desirable

* Copyright © 1966 by Music Music Music Inc.

that every team member speak a second language. This
was a cinch for the foreigners and no trouble for me. While
my English marks had been poor in school, foreign languages came easy. I had some Spanish from New Mexico
and considerable Japanese from my Air Force service. As
a Special Forces trooper, I learned some German, French,
Vietnamese, and Bihnar, another language spoken in
Vietnam.

Special Forces training demands a special combination of brains and brawn. The physical part is an extension
of what you have already been through in basic and airborne training. Judo and karate are part of it, and if you
have learned some of this already, you are that much
ahead of the others.

"On the starting command 'go,' " reads the instruction
for one of many tests, "begin running as fast as possible.
Run between the first two obstacles. Jump the six-foot
water ditch, run between the next two obstacles, and leap
the hurdle. Vault the fence and climb the wall by running-
jump-and-vault or hook-and-swing. Crawl through the
pipe tunnel. On your return, negotiate same obstacles in
reverse direction and start your second trip." There were
also mile runs that had to be done in eight and a half
minutes. I think the whole Army now has this dodge-run-
and-jump test.

There are lessons in raids, ambushes, evasion, and
escape, how to take weapons apart and put them together
in the dark, how to deal with adversaries in the night; instruction not only in being dropped into the jungle or sea

by plane but in how to be picked up again; special techniques for mountainside and underwater work. You get in a lot of these things in a two-week field-training exercise that concludes instruction.

On the brain side, everybody takes and must pass a two-week methods-of-instruction course before going into specialty training. This is to ensure that the trainee can pass along his knowledge to people who perhaps speak a different language. This involves practice in the use of interpreters and the making of training aids and tools. At Bragg, it is constantly emphasized that the success of Special Forces enterprises in foreign lands frequently depends upon winning local popular support.

To this end, everybody who goes through Bragg receives some instruction in propaganda and psychological warfare. This is an old but only recently appreciated activity. German generals wanted to shoot British airmen who dropped propaganda leaflets in World War I and did sentence some to hard labor. A World War II British air marshal called leaflets "pieces of bumph" and said the effect of dropping billions of them "was largely to supply the Continent's requirements for toilet paper for the five long years of war." But thousands of Italians and Germans gave up holding "surrender-pass" leaflets in their hands. Japan was bombed with everything, including the first atomic bombs, but finally surrendered to American propaganda leaflets. These fluttered into the courtyard of the Imperial Palace and were taken to Emperor Hirohito. He ordered the surrender and effected it by a radio broadcast. This had still been a topic of conversation when I was in Japan.

Bragg's instruction in propaganda covers leaflet writing, production in the field, and distribution by leaflet shells, rockets, and bombs. There is also instruction in radio broadcasting, tape recording, and the use of "hog-calling" loudspeakers and movie making for propaganda purposes. The leaflet writer, according to Bragg instructional material, "has the toughest selling job in the world. . . . Every facility at the disposal of the enemy, from domestic propaganda to military strength, is aimed at refuting his statements." The writer can only persuade; he must not ridicule or insult but should employ reason, logic, and emotional appeals. The format must be attractive or startling enough to get attention. The language must be correct, brief, and, above all, credible. Copy must have some relation to truth, the closer the better. This is our best asset in the word war.

The Special Forces insignia was originally a silver Trojan horse, worn on the beret over the left eye. It is now a design of arrows crossed behind a sword above *"De oppresso liber,"* Latin for "To liberate from oppression," and is worn on a flash of color on the beret just over the left eye. Officers and men of the Special Warfare Center have a special insignia of their own. It consists of a shield with a torch symbolizing light, liberty, and truth and a horse's head representing the knight in chess, the only piece capable of moving over others and striking inside enemy territory. A Latin motto, *"Veritas et Libertas,"* meaning "Truth and Freedom," adorns it. The white, gray, and black of the background symbolize the units' areas of activity. "White" propaganda is that in which the source is identified openly and honestly. "Black" is that giving a false source, perhaps an outright forgery of an order, a proclamation, or an enemy newspaper. "Gray" is in between, usually with no source at all given.

Training for the specialties is long and serious. Engineer and demolition trainees study mathematics for two weeks and engineering for eight weeks at Bragg and then go to the Engineer School at Fort Belvoir, Virginia, for an addition fourteen weeks. Communications trainees study sixteen weeks at Bragg. After completing an eight-week course at Bragg, some operations and intelligence trainees take the Intelligence Analysis Course at Fort Holabird, Maryland.

I had the choice of medicine or communications. Other classes were full. I chose medicine. Combat medics are most in demand and shortest in supply. The training has the longest schedule of all, a total of thirty-seven weeks. After going through the preliminaries at Bragg in the spring of 1963, I was sent again to San Antonio, where I had started Air Force training, to study medicine. This time I reported to Brooke Army Hospital and Medical Center at Fort Sam Houston. Conscientious objectors also study to be medical corpsmen there, but I didn't run into any of them.

Starting with simple things like blood typing and first aid, I studied hard at Brooke for twenty weeks. Emphasis was on the care of battlefield injuries and the hurts likely in airborne operations. While there are fewer of the latter than formerly, they can be serious. General Joe Stilwell, commander of the Special Forces until he was lost in a plane en route to Hawaii, for example, was badly hurt in a jump at Bragg. We also studied preventive medicine, the use of drugs, immunization, water supply and biological agents, jungle medical operatons, diagnosis and treatment of malaria, the care of children, even the delivery of babies. I helped dissect a dead dog and a human cadaver. You are not a doctor when you finish this, but you are better than a nurse for many injuries and diseases.

It was not all hard work at Brooke. I had my guitar along and in my spare time played and sang and worked on songs of my own. One a bit better than the others I called "Chains on a Man." It had to do with work, loneliness, and has the line "tomorrow comes and I'll be gone."

Emmett Harvey "Tex" Horn, a colorful medic trainee in the class ahead, liked the song and urged me to add more verses. In his spare time, Tex wrote science fiction and in high school had written plays and songs, so I was greatly encouraged by his praise. He was also an outdoorsman, a hunter, fisherman, rodeo rider, and an amateur parachute jumper. Tex lived in the next barracks, and I saw a lot of him. We had a lot of fun. Out of uniform, he wore blue jeans and a big straw hat. He was from Vidor, a small place near Beaumont, Texas. His father was a barber, and Tex had six brothers and sisters.

Robert Macdonald from Napa, California, a member of my own class, also encouraged my songwriting. He was known as El Flaco, the Skinny One, a nickname that he had acquired on weekend trips to Nuevo Laredo, across the Mexican border. He was a few years older, had been in the Army since 1952, and had served in Korea. "Why don't you write a song about us?" asked Macdonald as we were splitting a bottle of tequila in a San Antonio night spot one May evening in 1963.

I picked up my guitar and in a quarter of an hour or so came up with the original version of "The Ballad of the Green Berets." I started the chorus with the line about which I had been thinking, "Silver wings upon their chests," and continued with "these are men, America's best. One hundred men we'll test today, but only three win the green beret." These survived unchanged.

A verse paid tribute to Sergeant James Gabriel of Honolulu, one of the first Special Forces men to go to Vietnam. He was advising a small South Vietnamese force near the village of An Chau, seven miles from Da Nang, when the Viet Cong attacked in force just before dawn on April 8, 1962.

"I saw Sergeant Gabriel phoning and shooting and changing clips all at the same time," said a member of the command. "Three times he was wounded and knocked down. The third time he didn't get up." His last message to the U.S. base at Da Nang said: "Under heavy attack from all sides. Completely encircled by enemy. Ammunition expended. We are being overrun."

He and Sergeant Wayne E. Marchand of Plattsmouth, Nebraska, stayed behind to provide covering fire as the main body withdrew to shelter. They were overrun, wounded, and captured. When the Vietnamese troops counterattacked, the Viet Cong murdered Gabriel and Marchand. They were found with their hands tied behind their backs, dead from bullets in the head.

Gabriel is honored at Fort Bragg as the first Special Forces soldier to be killed in Vietnam. As you pass through the rustic arched gateway of a demonstration area named for him by order of Major General William P. Yarborough, former commander of the Special Warfare Center, you see carved in a tree stump these lines:

IN HONOR OF

JAMES GABRIEL, JR.

A SPECIAL FORCES SOLDIER

WHO DIED DEFENDING FREEDOM

IN THE

REPUBLIC OF VIETNAM

8 APRIL 1962

"Remember, Gabriel died on Asia's shore," I wrote. "To a wife and child, he'll return no more. They heard this man say, 'I would give my life for the green beret.'"

At the suggestion of my skinny friend Robert Macdonald, I sent my lines with four dollars to the Library of Congress and obtained a copyright. He says he kept me from "throwing the song away." Nobody was eager to buy it, but I sang it on leave in some Mexican-border and San Antonio night spots and earned considerable applause.

The four dollars eventually proved to be a great investment.

One day at lunch in the Brooke mess hall, a big place where women as well as men ate, I noticed a slender young WAC with a high hairdo under her chef's hat dishing out mashed potatoes. She handed me mine with a smile. On her tag, I read "Edelman," a name that could be German. "*Sprechen Sie Deutsch?*" I asked.

"*Nein,*" she replied.

Her name was Lavona Edelman. She was nineteen, pretty, and not German but a Pennsylvania Dutch girl from Lehighton, Pennsylvania. After graduation from high school there, she had enlisted in the Women's Army Corps at Wilkes-Barre, Pennsylvania, had taken basic training at Anniston, Alabama, and was studying operating-room nursing at Brooke.

After a little salesmanship on my part, she and a WAC friend named Charlotte, forgot about tentative dates they had for the evening. I picked up my guitar and two buddies, one of them Bob McDowell, at the barracks, and the five of us that evening drove in a little Triumph car to Brackenridge Park. This is a big park that is to San Antonio what Central Park is to New York City. There are gardens, lakes, and bridges. I carried Lavona's 110 pounds over one of these. I played and sang "The Ballad," "Chains on a Man," and some more songs on which I was working. It was a gay evening.

"I'll see you at breakfast," I told Lavona, and we parted. And I did, in the Brooke mess hall, where we both ate our meals. We began to date. She liked my songs and suggested subjects for more.

A private first class, even when he has extra airborne pay, is not supposed to think of marriage, and their officers frown on WAC's getting married. Overseas they must get consent of their commanding officers. But I decided that I wanted to marry Lavona and, since we were both expecting orders that would send us to other posts, that it had better be soon.

She refused several times, but one evening when we happened to meet on post at a giant garbage can, called the Dempsey Dumpster, she capitulated. She not only agreed to marry me but said that I didn't have to give her a wedding ring, that "a cigar band would do fine."

Her commanding officer didn't like it at all, but we were married by a local justice of the peace on July 18, 1963, just five weeks after we met. I gave her my silver parachutist's ring as a wedding ring.

General Eisenhower, they tell you in San Antonio, remembers Fort Sam Houston with affection because he reported there as a bridegroom. He had more time than I did. After only a night and two days together, Lavona was ordered to Fort Gordon, outside Atlanta, Georgia, and I was sent to Fort Jackson, South Carolina, for the next part of my Special Forces medical training. Only fourteen of a class of sixty-five passed the course. I was lucky enough to be one of them.

Vietnam

7 LAVONA AND I NEXT SAW each other two months later in Georgia. By then we were pretty frantic. I had completed my on-the-job training at the Army hospital at Fort Jackson and was returning to Fort Bragg for eight weeks of advanced medical training. She wanted to be with me and to continue in the Army, which she loved too. She filled out a lot of 1049 forms asking transfer to Bragg, but she had no luck. She had done so well in the operating-room training at Fort Gordon that her bosses wanted to keep her there.

She got to Bragg to be with me on my twenty-third birthday, November 1, 1963. To avoid the possibility of AWOL complications, she told the authorities where she was going and brought along her uniform and identity cards. She was my best and almost my only birthday present. Fort Gordon forgave her for whatever was involved, granted her leave and, at her request, a few weeks later an "excellent-conduct" discharge.

We bought a little Ford Falcon and set up housekeeping in Fayetteville. Money was scarce, and we lived first in a trailer and then in a tiny apartment. One month I sold a prized Mauser pistol for $80 to pay the rent and bills. While some soldiers send money home every month and buy savings bonds, enough are always short of cash to support a drive-in pawnshop on Bragg Boulevard, which runs from the post to Fayetteville.

President Kennedy was so close to the Special Forces that his assassination that month was stunning news at

Fort Bragg. I first heard of it in a medical class, which was at once dismissed. Everything stopped. Flags were half-staffed. The Special Forces troopers were too tough for tears, but we gathered angrily around television sets, frustrated because there was nothing we could do to change what had happened.

Next day word came that Mrs. Kennedy wanted the Special Forces to take part in the funeral services. Everybody at Bragg was touched that she took the time to think of us amid all the pressure on her. Colonel William P. Grieves, deputy commander of the Special Warfare Center, three officers, and forty-three of the best-looking and most senior enlisted men of the Fifth, Sixth, and Seventh Special Forces started at once for Washington. I was then attached to the Seventh but had neither the seniority nor the looks for this detail.

Our Green Berets took turns with servicemen from Fort Myer, Virginia, and elsewhere guarding the body of President Kennedy in the Capitol Rotunda on Sunday. Cots for the troopers were set up in the Capitol basement. At Arlington Cemetery the next day, the Special Forces men formed an honor guard from the horse-drawn gun caisson to the grave on the green hillside.

After the final graveside ceremonies—a jet-plane fly-by, a twenty-one gun salute, and the heart-wrenching notes of taps—Sergeant Major Francis Ruddy of the Special Forces took the green beret from his own head and placed it on President Kennedy's grave next to the eternal flame. Others added Army, Navy, and Air Force hats and insignia of the Old Guard, 1st Battalion, 3rd Infantry, of Fort Myer. It was soon decided that the Special Warfare Center, for which a new building was under construction, should be named for President Kennedy.

I completed my medical training, took part in several realistic field-training exercises, won my stripes and the right to wear my own green beret. It was a proud moment, but there was no ceremony. In contrast to the noise and shouting of airborne training, the whole Special Forces operation was quiet and serious. Much of the work was highly confidential. The men were older, and most were married. The emphasis was on teamwork.

After going through field exercises together, any member of an "A" team, either officer or enlisted man, had the right to blackball any other member right out of the detachment. This sometimes happened. Of the first hundred troopers picked for South Vietnam, I was told that only thirty-two survived the blackballing.

Interest increased in South Vietnam. Only one American soldier, Army Specialist Fourth Class James T. Davis of Livingston, Tennessee, had died in combat there in 1961. He had been killed when a convoy hit a land mine and was ambushed. Thirty-two Americans, however, were killed there in 1962 and seventy-seven in 1963. The Special Forces studied jungle warfare in Panama and also at Bragg. Replicas of Vietnamese villages were erected for this at Bragg and later at Fort Polk, Louisiana; Camp Bullis, Texas; Fort Jackson, South Carolina; Fort Devens, Massachusetts; and elsewhere.

There was trouble also in the Congo. By the middle of 1964, I was in the Third Special Forces Group, attached to the surgeon's office. We were studying the problems of Africa. Half a dozen college professors, including some native Nigerians and one who had taught at the University of the Sudan in Khartoum, lectured us on all sorts of subjects. Several of my classmates at this time later saw service in the Congo, Ethiopia, Mali, and Iraq. There are Special Forces groups for Asia, Latin America, Europe, the Middle East, and Africa.

On my own time, I continued to play my guitar and work on my songs. I earned a $600 reenlistment bonus by signing up for three more years and spent part of it for a recorder of my own and began to play my songs into it. This tape recorder—which cost only $98, as I recall—proved the best investment of my life.

Through my Third Special Forces service, I met Second Lieutenant Gerald Gitell of Boston. He was a public-information officer for the group and took a professional and also a personal interest in my songs. He sent them to a lot of people and took me with him to New York and Boston in an effort to sell them. We had no luck. At this time a song titled "The Green Beret March" appeared. The words were by Phyllis Fairbanks. The music was the work of Ken Whitcomb, chief arranger for the West Point band. Major General William P. Yarborough, commander of the Special Warfare Center, liked the march and gave it official approval. The words are:

When you see a man wearing the green beret,
You know that you've seen one of the best.
Pride in his stride shows he's passed the test,
And is one of the great fighting men
Towering high above the rest.
Whenever men who are men gather in peace or war,
You'll see Green Berets
Open the door to life in a force,
A very special new force,
*You'll find that men wear the green beret.**

Gerry Gitell believed the people behind the march would be logical prospects for my ballad, which we were than calling "The Ballad of the Green Beret." He talked to General Yarborough's office about it and obtained a name and address from Lieutenant Tom Koentop, General Yarborough's aide. The name was that of Chester Gierlach, partner of Miss Fairbanks in a New York company, Music Music Music Inc.

On June 17, 1964, Lieutenant Gitell mailed two of my tapes, a sheet of ordinary typing paper with the lyrics, and a one-page letter to Gierlach. One tape was the original version of "The Ballad." The other was a "sad tale 'bout a brave young trooper whose chute did fail." This was called "Trooper's Fall" and eventually appeared as "Trooper's Lament."

In his letter, Gitell explained that the singer, a Spe-

* Copyright © 1963 by Music Music Music Inc.

cial Forces medic, had written the songs, that Special Forces men were interested in "The Ballad," and that the commander of the Special Warfare Center had approved it. The Fort Bragg bookstore was eager to sell it in any form. Gitell wrote that on a trip home to Boston, he had found that people "in a completely unmilitary environment" approved the ballad.

Gierlach was interested. Music Music Music Inc. would do what it could with the tapes, and I assigned my copyright on "The Ballad" to the company. The judge advocate's office at Bragg looked over the contract and approved. I was greatly encouraged. I felt so grateful to Gerry Gitell that I gave him a twenty-five percent share in any royalties as a writer that I might receive on "The Ballad." But recording companies and music publishers were not frantic for military ballads in 1964. The most popular song was "I Want to Hold Your Hand," as sung by some long-haired young Englishmen. Many weary months passed, and Gerry Gitell was out of the service before there were any royalties.

We began to hear more about Vietnam at Bragg, especially after August 2 and 4, when North Vietnamese patrol torpedo boats attacked U.S. Navy destroyers *Maddox* and *C. Turner Joy* in the Gulf of Tonkin. President Johnson ordered air raids on North Vietnam in retaliation. More Special Forces troopers were sent to South Vietnam to combat infiltrators from the north. It was a gradual thing. At first there were just a few requests for volunteers, "six weapons men, four medics for Vietnam." Then we heard one day in the surgeon's office that practically the entire Fifth Special Forces Group was to ship out by the end of the year.

"Quite a few of us are going over," a friend told me. "Lieutenant Jimmy Walker and some others you know. Do you want to come along with us?"

"Well, I guess you are going to get me, anyway," I answered. "And at the rate things are going, I'll probably never make it to Africa."

Lavona and I drove out to the post a couple of weeks later to pick up some papers. There at the top of a list of names was: "Specialist-5 Barry Sadler, reassigned Fifth Special Forces, Vietnam." I received my orders, dropped out of the Africa area studies, and processed out of the Third Special Forces Group and into the Fifth.

This just involved going up the road a quarter of a mile, checking into another headquarters, and changing the color of the flash on my green beret. Each group was a different color. I had worn a red one with the Seventh; a red, black, yellow, and white quadrant with the Third; and now, in the Fifth, a black one with a white border.

I was assigned to a "B" team as a medic. In Special Forces, a "B" team is a field-headquarters support group providing replacements and supplies for perhaps ten twelve-man "A" teams organized and operated as I have described. A captain usually commands an "A" team and a major a "B" team. The commander of our team was Major Mitchell Sakey from Boston. Sergeant Major Robert Frander, a veteran of three combat parachute jumps, was the ranking sergeant. The other medic was Sergeant Billy Britt.

We were issued gear and weapons—machine guns, mortars, recoilless rifles. We studied booby traps and practiced demolition. We were given briefings and books on Vietnam. Some of these traced its history back two thousand years to the legendary origin of the people as children of the union of a dragon and a goddess, recounted their struggles with the Chinese, the French, and the Japanese, and explained the promises and obligations that required Americans to help "those oppressed," as my ballad put it.

The printed matter and every instructor emphasized nine rules of conduct for soldiers joining the U.S. Military Assistance Command at Vietnam. They were the following:

"Remember we are special guests; we make no demands and seek no special treatment.

"Join with the people! Understand their life, use phrases from their language, and honor their customs and laws.

"Treat women with politeness and respect.

"Make personal friends among the soldiers and common people.

"Always give the Vietnamese the right of way.

"Be alert to security and ready to react with your military skill.

"Don't attract attention by loud, rude, or unusual behavior.

"Avoid separating yourself from the people by a display of wealth or privilege.

"Above all else you are members of the U.S. military forces on a difficult mission, responsible for all your official and personal actions. Reflect honor upon yourself and the United States of America."

I had four weeks or so of classes at Bragg in the Vietnamese language. This is like Chinese in several respects, but it is a little easier because the alphabet is Roman, like ours, with variations. Like Chinese, Vietnamese is a tonal language, the same vowels pronounced in a different tone have a different meaning. The word *ma*, for example, has six different meanings, and none of them mother, depending on the way the "a" is sounded. There are accents and other marks to indicate pronunciation. These tonal variations give the Vietnamese a thirty-nine letter alphabet. The time was short, but I learned several hundred words of the language, including *bac-si*, which means "doctor" or "medic."

In November, I made a will leaving everything to Lavona and also assigned my power of attorney to her. More Americans were then being killed in Washington, D.C., traffic accidents than in the Vietnam fighting, but it would have been foolish not to consider the possibility of my death. Practically all soldiers make wills, but many, for one reason or another, balk at giving their wives power of attorney. This omission can cause their families difficulties if the soldiers are captured or listed as missing, despite all the help the services provide. I wanted to spare Lavona all worry possible. Her father had died a few weeks earlier, and she was pregnant.

All members of the "B" team were preparing to leave, and their wives and girls had a big farewell party upstairs at the Noncommissioned Officers Club of the 82nd Airborne one evening toward the end of the month. I brought Lavona. Major Sakey and his wife were present. I remember particularly Sergeant Horace E. Young and his Japanese wife, named Ei. Young was thirty-four, a little older than many of us. He had been born in Aledo and had lived in Moline, Illinois. He had served earlier with Special Forces in Germany.

I played my guitar and sang "The Ballad" and several other songs. There were some cheers and also some tears. The party gradually broke up, most of the men not to see one another again until actual departure for Vietnam.

My wife and I expected to have the baby at Bragg, and I planned to take mother and child home to Lavona's family in Pennsylvania and get them settled before shipping out. But the baby was late. Several days went by and we could wait no longer.

On the morning of December 2, 1964, we went down to the hospital for a final check. Nothing seemed imminent, so I piled Lavona, the tape recorder, and our few personal belongings into the Falcon and sped northward on Highway 95. We drove out of North Carolina, across Virginia, around Washington, D.C., and stopped for dinner at a roadside restaurant near Baltimore.

Lavona ate a big meal, roast beef or something like

that. As we drove into Pennsylvania through Lancaster and Reading, she became uncomfortable but still had no regular pains.

"It would be good practice for me to deliver this baby," I told her as we passed Allentown. She wasn't enthusiastic about the idea.

We rolled up to the Edelman home on North Fifth Street in Lehighton at 9 P.M. Lavona had some more pains, and around 11 P.M. I took her to the Gnaden Hutten Hospital. I hung around there a while, but nothing seemed to be happening, so I went back to the Edelmans' and went to sleep.

The hospital telephoned me sometime in the morning. "Congratulations," said a voice. "You are the father of a fine baby boy."

And he was too, the finest-looking kid in the hospital, I thought when I pulled myself together and had my first look at him a few hours later.

We called him Thor. I had happened to read about the Scandinavian god of thunder and his hammer. I thought Thor a good, strong name for a boy, and Lavona agreed.

I had to leave the day after Lavona and Thor came home from the hospital, and she drove me to the bus station. We were cheerful until I said in parting, as I had at each good-bye since we'd met at Fort Sam Houston, "See you at breakfast." This broke her up.

As I wasn't likely to be so near New York for a while, I detoured there on my way back and visited Music Music

Music Inc., then in an office at 1667 Broadway. It was a fairly new firm, formed by former advertising-agency people originally to publish their own songs. Chet Gierlach had been music director at McCann-Erickson, and Phyllis Fairbanks had been a copywriter at J. Walter Thompson. She had started writing songs as a student at Cornell University.

With a new son to look out for, I hoped for some money as an advance against royalties on my songs, but they had not been recorded or published, and there was nothing due me. The leading folk-music album at the time was *Another Side of Bob Dylan,* which had to do with gypsy girls and "cracked country lips." The public had not shared General Yarborough's enthusiasm for "The Green Beret March," and its sales were modest. But Gierlach was hopeful. If I taped any new songs in Vietnam, he wanted me to send them to him.

Back at Bragg, I engaged in some scrounging all over the post for medical items and technical manuals that might be hard to get in Vietnam. We heard that Merck manuals and similar books were scarce there. I used the old trade-and-barter system in getting ready. At the last minute, a reminder came around that there would be fun as well as fighting and that we should take cameras, transistor radios, and other personal items. I decided to take along my guitar.

On Christmas Eve, I read in the newspapers that "Tex" Horn, my good friend of Fort Sam Houston in 1964, had been killed the day before in Vietnam. We'd had many

Here's how I looked as a kid, a picture taken of me in Las Vegas.

My mother, whose name before she was married was Bebe Littlefield, came from Phoenix, Arizona.

The guitar I accompany myself with today is one of several instruments I learned to play as a boy.

I compete in a judo tournament at March Air Force Base.

At Fort Benning, mass parachute drops like this were a part of our training.

A Special Forces trooper rappels down from the top of a tower used for instruction in rock climbing at Fort Bragg, North Carolina.

Here is the Special Forces team that I was a part of at Nha Trang in 1965. *First row, left to right:* Capt. Len M. Hanawald, Lieut. Vincent E. Stahl, Capt. Roland M. Schick, Maj. Mitchell A. Sakey, Capt. Philip Arsenault, Capt. Stanley M. Clough, Sgt. Major Robert Frander. *Second row:* M/Sgt Robert E. Gabe, Sgt. Horace Young (killed in action at Song Be), Sgt. Daniel C. Martinez, Corp. Richard S. Bartlett, Sergeants Muzquiz, Sadler, Charles D. Crockett, Pete Carasco. *Back row:* Sergeants Paul P. Troyan, Aldege Martin, Arthur M. Campo, Forrest E. Todd, Richard C. Ryan, Billy Britt, Paul R. O'Krusky. Eighteen returned home with Purple Heart decorations.

This carved drummer beside a thatched house gives you an idea how primitive the people are in the area where the Special Forces were sent deep in the mountains of Vietnam.

This weaver keeps the warp taut by lashing one end of the primitive loom about the waist.

Every one of the Bihnars in the front row is a man. One of them makes a sign with his fingers to ward off the evil spirit in the camera.

As a medic with the Special Forces, I had many opportunities to help the South Vietnamese people among whom we lived. This woman brought her sick baby to me one day. I fixed him up.

A patrol of Montagnards I took into the jungle near Plei Do Lim in the mountains of Vietnam.

We take a break to study the map and try to figure out where we are.

Patrol strikes out into the Central Highlands.

I interrogate a couple of prisoners captured on the Ayun River.

That's Sgt. Fred Wright on the left. He wears a Montagnard bracelet on his wrist, a way of showing these people that we were sincerely their friends.

Sgt. Wright found this prisoner pretty tight lipped.

I wouldn't exactly call it gustatory delight, but the Montagnards who went on patrol with us taught us to eat some unusual dishes. This giant lizard went into the pot.

So did this python.

And here a native soldier and I share a meal of rice balls and fish.

There was no alternative: this Viet Cong village had to be put to the torch. The figure turned toward us is one of my buddies who was killed in Vietnam.

Capt. Chandler Robbins III of San Antonio (in the beret), Sgt. Billy Bean (the tall man), and some fellow officers at Camp Hardy, Plei Do Lim, 1965.

A patrol pushing through tall dry grass of the Vietnamese Central Highlands set afire by shelling. You can see the flames licking at the boots of the man in the lead.

S/Sgt Bill LeGrand of Ohio, who was fatally injured at Plei Do Lim.

Thor Johnston, a 220-pound demolition expert from Eureka, California, fiddles with a massive shootin' iron while drinking a beer and getting his hair cut at Plei Do Lim.

Another fallen buddy was Sgt. Raymond Vrba.

This is the last picture of my friend Sgt. Emmett "Tex" Horn. Look into those eyes and see for yourself what it means to be a combat infantryman in Vietnam today. The day is the day after Christmas, 1964. The funeral is for Sgt. Horn, whose death is recalled in the lyrics of my song "I'm a Lucky One."

Back home from the war, I concentrate on trying to get the public to listen to my song "The Ballad of the Green Berets."

The break finally comes. This is one of my first recording sessions, and that's my music publisher, Chet Gierlach, setting the beat.

The strain of getting a song exactly right for an album shows plainly in this picture taken during a recording session at RCA's studios in New York City.

This is the first picture I ever saw of our baby. Lavona sent it to me in Vietnam.

My son Thor was the inspiration for "Lullaby." We tricked him out as a miniature Green Beret.

things in common. He also had married a WAC, a pretty
girl named Susan Blasko, of Carmichaels, Pennsylvania,
whom he had met in San Antonio. He had gone out as a
medic to the First Special Forces group at Okinawa and
had been given temporary duty with the Fifth in Vietnam.

A patrol that he was leading near Ashau was ambushed and took cover. After a brief fire fight, he raised his
head to look around. A sniper's bullet hit him in the head,
and he died in the helicopter evacuating him to a hospital. He had been awarded the Silver Star and a Republic
of Vietnam citation and received a posthumous Purple
Heart. Poor Tex. He left the manuscripts of a couple of
novels.

On December 27, in rain, four teams of troopers with
all our gear piled into a big KC-135 jet transport at a
field near Bragg and flew nonstop to Travis Air Force Base,
near San Francisco. We unloaded for a few hours there
while the plane was refueled, then flew to Hawaii, where
we stretched our legs and spent the night.

As one GI passing another, I met Sergeant William F.
LeGrand, another Special Forces medic, that evening for
the first time. He was on his way from Vietnam to his
home in Lima, Ohio, on emergency leave. We had much
in common. He had been born and grew up in the coal-
mining town of Luzerne, a suburb of Wilkes-Barre, Pennsylvania. He enlisted at seventeen and finished high school
in the Army. He was in the Korean War at nineteen and
had tours in Iceland, Japan, and Germany before joining
the Special Forces. He had trained at Sam Houston and

Bragg. He had a wife named Beverly and two little daughters in Ohio. The younger, the survivor of premature twins, had been born only the previous June. He expected to return to Vietnam shortly.

"See you on Tu Do Street!" he called as we said goodnight. Duong Tu Do, Freedom Street, is the principal street through the fashionable shopping, theater, bar, and café area of Saigon, the capital of South Vietnam, a city often called the Paris of the East.

We took off at 5 A.M. next day, stopped at Wake Island long enough to stretch our legs on the beach and to drink some beer and Cokes, then zoomed into Clark Air Force Base, near Manila in the Philippines. We were put up at the transit barracks. There we put on civilian slacks and shirts and spent the evening at the Noncommissioned Officers Club. Next day we flew on west.

The FASTEN SEAT BELTS sign was flashed on, and Major Sakey, who had been riding with the pilots and crew up front, came back to his seat. "We are ten miles out and making our approach to Saigon," he told us.

"Oh boy!" I said, looking out through a tiny window at the jungle for the first time.

Medic to the Montagnards

8 WE LANDED at the Saigon airport at about 8:30 A.M. It was hot. We were issued weapons and had to unload our gear for another change of planes. As the South Vietnam government was having a crisis and a Saigon hotel quartering U.S. officers had been bombed only a few days before, everybody was viewed suspiciously, especially if he carried a bag or a package. Most of us stayed outside on the field taking turns guarding the gear. There were all sorts of uniforms and berets of several colors around the airport.

After a seven-hour wait, during which we were not allowed to leave the area, we flew north that same evening, December 29, about 198 miles up the coast to Nha Trang and the Special Forces headquarters. We unloaded, checked in, and were assigned quarters.

In the middle of the night, I was aroused by the crackle of small-arms fire, the first shots I had ever heard fired in anger. They came from outside the camp perimeter. I grabbed my M-16 rifle, but we were ordered to stay in our quarters because we didn't know the place. Our people beat off the attackers without casualties.

Our arrival brought the number of Special Forces troopers in South Vietnam to fourteen hundred. This was double the total six months earlier. We had one camp at Duong Dong, on Phu Quoc Island, twenty miles off the coast to the southwest in the Gulf of Thailand. Captain Joe Parent was killed there. But most camps were in the northern and western provinces and located with a view toward preventing infiltration of enemy guerrillas and supplies from the north and from Laos and Cambodia to the west. We had a camp at Kham Duc, atop a hill where the late President Ngo Dinh Diem had cleared an airstrip and started building his summer palace. This was forty-three miles southwest of Da Nang.

General William C. Westmoreland commanded only 23,000 American servicemen in South Vietnam at the start of 1965. There were 15,000 soldiers, 850 Marines, 1,150 sailors, and 6,000 airmen. All were advisers, and technically we were not at war. Not until later that year was the American flag flown alongside the South Vietnam flag at installations where our men served. Colonel John H. Spears was the Special Forces commander in Vietnam.

After two days at Nha Trang, during which we were paid and issued more gear, my team was flown by a twin-engine Caribou plane to Pleiku. This is a town of seven thousand population at the intersection of the important east-west Highway 19 and north-south Highway 14. These were much fought over supply routes in the Central Highlands. At Pleiku were a corps headquarters of the South Vietnamese Army; Camp Holloway, a U.S. airfield; and headquarters of a Special Forces "C" team. As "A" teams report to "B" teams, the latter report to "C" teams.

The Viet Cong were known to have snipers all around watching for low-flying aircraft. To foil them, the Caribou came down to the red earth in a steep dive, reversed its propellers, and blew red dust all over the place. A man riding a weapons carrier protected by sandbags took us to the "C" team. We were issued more weapons and briefed.

My first assignment was as relief medic at Special Forces camps around Pleiku. They were mostly in places too small to be found on maps. There was a rabies scare at Camp Plei Tanang Le, forty-five miles to the east. I helped take over while several men who had been scratched by the dog were flown out for preventive treatment. My first patient was a man with shrapnel wounds in the leg and a *punji* stick through his foot. He recovered. I ran the dispensary and took care of sick call there for several days. It was my first medic work entirely on my own.

Later we had another rabies scare at a different camp when a rat bit Sergeant Billy Bean on the nose while he slept. He awoke mad as a horned toad and had to be flown out. The possibility of rabies is serious at any time, but when the bite is close to the brain, every minute counts in prevention.

I was given a sudden change of orders and sent to Camp Soui Doi, thirty miles or so east of Pleiku. A few weeks later, on February 22, a convoy was ambushed six kilometers east of Mangyang Pass, and nearly everybody was wiped out. Second Lieutenant Leslie D. Griggs was shot through the back and neck. The Viet Cong attackers rolled him over and thought he was dead. While they were looting the vehicles, he crawled to a radio set and called in an air strike on them. After the air strike beat off the VC, he stayed on the radio and directed helicopters in to pick up the wounded. He was recommended for the Medal of Honor and received the Distinguished Service Cross.

Sergeant Long, a medic, who had been in training

with me, was seriously wounded a little later at the same camp. The VC were so strong then in the area that both Highway 14 and Highway 19 were closed to traffic for several weeks. The winding hundred miles of the latter from Pleiku east to Qui Nhon was literally a highway of death. A company of South Vietnamese Rangers and U.S. Special Forces caught at Mangyang Pass on this road was rescued by helicopter after two American jet strikes blasted the VC off the adjoining cliffs.

Soui Doi was a new camp where South Vietnam government, with American help, was relocating Montagnards from the Ban Me Thuot area, a hundred miles to the south. Hundreds were being moved, mostly by truck, in an effort to end the grievances that had caused three thousand of them to revolt in a war-within-a-war a few months earlier. I later had Montagnards as patients and soldiers at Pleiku, Kontum, Plei Do Lim, and many other places. I gradually learned a lot about them and found them brave, intelligent, good fighters. They were important in the war, and they were also a lot of fun. I always enjoyed working with them.

Montagnard is a French word meaning "mountaineer." The Montagnards are the hillbillies of Vietnam. We called them Yards for short. They are not Vietnamese, Chinese, or Cambodian but an aboriginal Malaysian people. They are muscular, a little bigger and better built than the Vietnamese, who consider them inferior and refer to them as *moîs*, meaning "baboons" or "savages." There are more than nine hundred thousand of them in perhaps a hundred tribes. The principal tribes are the Rhade and the Bihnar. I learned to speak some Bihnar.

Montagnards have only local loyalties and regard people in a village twenty miles away as foreigners. They wear their hair long over their shoulders, have brass earrings and brass necklaces and loincloths. The men wear black vests. The women are often bare-breasted and wear a short handwoven skirt with tribal colors in the cloth. Both men and women file their teeth, sometimes to a point. I had to pull a lot of them. They like to have gold teeth put in, sometimes with a little pink-plastic heart, which they find very pretty. A lot of them are animists, or spirit believers. They worship the spirits of the field, the stream, and the rocks or of their ancestors.

They sacrifice animals to appease the spirits. Some chop off the heads of their enemies with a machetelike sword. They eat dogs and cats. I would often see a dead dog stretched on a rock and a Montagnard skinning him. They ferment a rice wine and mix it with buffalo blood. Some tribesmen are alcoholics, and there is a lot of cirrhosis of the liver. Some tribes are ruled by women, who can be very free or very rigid. Older women chew betel nuts until their gums are black. Some of them smoke Cambodian tobacco, which has narcotic qualities, through bamboo water pipes.

Many Montagnards have never seen a wheeled vehicle. They are ignorant but not stupid. They catch on fast and mechanically are fantastic. Pull a fellow out of the hills who has never seen anything but a crossbow, tell him he is a mechanic and to go to work in the motor pool, and pretty soon you'll hear him down there tearing down a motor.

To protect the Montagnards from lowlanders, the French practically made the Central Highlands a tribal reservation. After they departed in 1954, lowlanders began to push the Montagnards deeper into the forests, and old frictions began anew. In 1962, our Special Forces teams began to arm and train them to fight the Communist guerrillas. At first the Montagnards were given guns, drilled for two weeks, and allowed to go home. Later they were organized as strike-force battalions that served by contract for six months to two years under South Vietnamese commanders advised by Americans, at first mostly Special Forces teams. The strike-force organization is separate from the Army of the Republic of Vietnam (ARVIN) and the Regional Force, formerly known as the Civil Guard.

Three flares shot into the air from a VC-held mountain signaled the start of the Montagnard revolt on the night of September 19, 1964. Three thousand tribesmen at camps in Bu Prang, Bon Sar Pa, Ban Don, and Buon Mi Ga revolted, killed twenty-nine Vietnamese soldiers, captured a hundred more, and seized a score of Americans as hostages. They marched on Ban Me Thuot, a provincial capital, and captured a radio station at its edge.

The bravery and ingenuity of Captain Vernon W. Gillespie, Jr., of Lawton, Oklahoma, commander of the Special Forces "A" team there, prevented the revolt of seven hundred more Montagnards, members of the Rhade tribe, at Buon Brieng, a few miles north of Ban Me Thuot. Gillespie took command of the camp. He, the ranking Rhade officer, and the Vietnamese commander then donned native costumes, called in a sorcerer, sacrificed a pig and three chickens, and the three became blood brothers in the Rhade tribe. The Montagnards at Buon Brieng remained loyal.

Captain Gillespie then drove to Ban Me Thuot and joined Colonel John F. Freund, who was an adviser from the II Corps headquarters, and Major Edwin E. Brooks, Special Forces commander in the area, in arguing the thousand armed Montagnards there into abandoning the revolt and returning to their camps. Major Brooks led out those holding the radio station. Speaking fluent French, Colonel Freund reminded the leaders of America's friendship and aid to the Rhade.

"Who will now continue this role?" he asked. "Where will you get rice and clothing and medicine?" He warned them that the Vietnamese would bomb them if they remained at Ban Me Thout and asked, "Who of you will be responsible for the blood of these men?" All returned to their camps. Freund has since been promoted to brigadier general.

Demands of the rebels that all Vietnamese leave the highlands and that a free Montagnard state be set up were rejected. But they were promised better and safer camps, more schools and medical help, and a greater proportion of Americans among their advisers. That's why I was sent to Camp Soui Doi. The Rhade tribesmen moved there were homesick for their old lands in Darlac Province and refused to fight in Mangyang Pass, and the camp eventually was closed.

Because they were shelters for the Viet Cong, we had to destroy some villages in South Vietnam in 1965. Snipers in Cam Ne, just two miles from the Da Nang air base, for example, shot so many Marines there that the village had to be burned. A television camera recorded this, and a lot of people got the idea that this was all Americans were doing in Vietnam. Nothing could be further from the truth.

For every village destroyed by Americans, at least a dozen have been built or rebuilt. I know because I was there. Sites for several have been bulldozed right out of the forest around Gia Nghia in Quang Duc, the most sparsely populated province of South Vietnam, and new five-family houses were built. Montagnard villagers, their animals, and all their gear were trucked there.

At the various Montagnard camps, I treated or helped treat between 950 and 1,500 people a month for almost every conceivable type of disease. Eight people died of plague at Kontum. I saw lepers, treated cases of cholera and typhus, cut abscesses out of spines, pulled teeth, and delivered babies. Delivery of a baby was the simplest thing in the world. We just stood around to see that nothing went wrong.

At Soui Doi we built a new camp around the old ARVIN regimental headquarters. There were reports of Viet Cong all around us but no fire fights while I was there.

A tiger prowled the perimeter and one night came into camp. One of the guys saw him and took a shot. The whole camp woke up thinking it was an attack. A lot of people were shooting, but the tiger loped away over the barbed wire and the minefields.

The jungle is no picnic, but it is not as hazardous as some people make out. Tigers generally scamper away as soon as they hear shooting. The pythons are no more dangerous, though some of them seem as long as railroad cars. There are some lizards as much as five feet long, but the Montagnards eat lizards and practically any other kind of meat. They aren't choosy, and after you are there for a while, you aren't either.

I've heard people say that all water in Vietnam is unsafe. The clear water in the mountains is as good as any, but you never know what's happening just upstream and can't afford to take chances. We purified the water with chlorine and iodine tablets, as well as by boiling it. The tablets give water such a taste that among the most welcome gifts for soldiers in Vietnam are packages of powdered Kool-Aid. One can be mailed in a letter. A lot of people don't realize it, but letters sent to men in South Vietnam via an APO address need only a five-cent stamp.

The saddest figure in camp in Vietnam is the fellow who doesn't turn out for mail call, who has nobody writing to him. Anything that doesn't rot or melt can be sent to soldiers in Vietnam. Fudge is out. It melts. Cookies may arrive moldy. Canned fruit and other canned foods are welcome. So are razor blades, tobacco, batteries for transistor radios. Governor George Romney made a lot of friends by seeing that seven thousand soldiers from Michigan received Christmas packages of the state's products. Personal mail is what is most desired—as long as a girl doesn't tell a guy what a great time she had with his best friend. Telephone calls across the Pacific are hard to make and costly. A fellow called his wife collect at the University of Arizona six times, and she had a bill of $1,084!

A daily salt pill protects the soldier against heat exhaustion (the temperature goes higher than a hundred degrees at times in some parts of the country). A weekly antimalaria pill guards him against the common forms of this disease. A falciparum type of malaria, against which usual remedies were ineffective, caused trouble, but a field team from the Walter Reed Army Institute of Research found that this form also can be controlled most of the time by a shiny white pill previously used in the treatment of leprosy. It is called DDS, short for diaminodiphenyl sulfone. This is just one useful medical advance to come out of the war.

I had to interrupt my work to become a patient myself and have surgical attention for an ignominious but extremely painful case of thrombosed hemorrhoids. The only thing pleasant about it was that it led to my meeting Lieutenant Colonel Margaret Clarke at the Eighth Field Hospital and the writing of "Salute to the Nurses."

Many soldiers became interested in helping the Montagnards. Under the leadership of Colonel William E. Bethea and Master Sergeant John Coache, a combat movie cameraman from Oakview, California, the Air Force's 34th Tactical Group at Bien Hoa Air Base induced residents of Santa Barbara, California, to donate thousands of toys for the children in the highland hamlets.

A former Special Forces officer at Dak Pek, on the Laos border, George Gaspard, who once played football for Louisiana State, became the Quang Duc province representative of the State Department's Agency for International Development. He directed the resettlement of some nine thousand Montagnards in the Gia Nghia area and coordinated aid from all U.S. agencies in the province.

He celebrated his fortieth birthday and his first year in the job with a party in a frame house a few yards from the jungle. Attending were five elephants, a wounded bear, various Montagnard chiefs and tribesmen, the governor, U.S. and Vietnamese soldiers, a girl wearing eight bracelets and nothing else, and George McArthur, an Associated Press correspondent who told the world about it.

Also present were three girls from the provincial propaganda team, whose love songs over the radio were supposed to pull the Viet Cong from the jungle, and a Vietnamese lieutenant who challenged everybody to judo by announcing, "Me black tiger."

First to arrive was Sergeant Edgar Alford, a lanky Army medic from De Funiak Springs, Florida.

"Doc," said Gaspard, "the first thing you have to do is give the bear a shot of penicillin."

"I ain't checked out on bears," objected Alford.

Two Montagnards had caught the bear in a trap, injuring its right paw, and had sold it the night before to Gaspard, who hoped some outfit would want it as a mascot.

Sergeant Thomas Gearheart from Murray, Kentucky, who had dealt with bears back home, and Sergeant Alford tied the bear down with rope and gave him enough penicillin to take care of the wounded paw. Alford then barbecued two goats and three pigs.

Gaspard served these along with a birthday cake, some American beer, three jugs of rice wine, and some champagne in paper cups to his vastly assorted guests. The Montagnards laid aside their spears and crossbows and gave everybody rides on the elephants. Life in Vietnam can be very interesting.

Saigon

9 I HELPED SET UP a Special Forces "B" team headquarters at Kontum, the capital of the mountain province of the same name to the north of Pleiku. The Pleiku–Qui Nhon highway had been reopened. First a 168-vehicle convoy and then one of 77 trucks came through from the coast under the escort of armored cars and helicopters. Some more men for our team came with them.

On our second day at Kontum we went out on patrol, and down by the river a Viet Cong fired a pistol at Sergeant Billy Britt. This gave us a chance to test our weapons. We fired machine guns, AR-15's, and our pistols, but whoever had fired got away.

New quarters were built for us. We prepared machine-gun bunkers, dug trenches, and filled sandbags. Kontum was a strategic point on Highway 14. There were rumors that the Viet Cong planned to capture the place and hold it for a fortnight during the monsoon season for the propaganda effect this would have.

On the lighter side, I found a pleasant NCO Club there and had the luck to win a few dollars shooting craps. Some Military Assistance Command people had a little leopard cub for a pet. He was a cute little nine pounds of wildcat. He wouldn't hurt you, but he liked to hide in the bushes and jump out at your boots, a little ball of fur spitting and making the most god-awful sound. He once jumped a pilot carrying a lot of gear—the gear went in every direction.

Dogs are the most popular pets in Vietnam. Many of

them are used for sentry duty and tracking the Viet Cong. But there are also pet monkeys and pet deer, tiny things. I later brought back from Pleiku a couple of small civet cats, very good for catching rats. These tree animals climb over everything.

The oddest pet probably was a six-foot boa constrictor named Clarence bought in a Portland, Oregon, pet shop by Lieutenant Jay E. Vaughn and smuggled ashore when the 2nd Brigade of the U.S. 4th Infantry landed at Qui Nhon. "I told the lady in the shop that we wanted a mascot adaptable to the climate," explained Vaughn. "She let me have Clarence at a reduced rate because he was going into battle. More than two thousand troops knew about him, but he was kept a secret from the Navy."

Most of the natives around Kontum were Montagnards. They liked us and Americans in general partly because of the medical work there of a woman physician, Dr. Patricia Smith from Seattle, Washington. The tribesmen called her Ya Pogang, meaning the "honorable lady of medicine."

Kontum has the highest leprosy rate in the world and a lot of tuberculosis. Dr. Smith was sent to Kontum in 1959 by the Catholic Relief Services, an agency of the National Catholic Welfare Conference, and first worked in a leprosarium operated by French nuns. She later opened a dispensary for children and in 1963 expanded this into the forty-bed Minh-Quy hospital, two miles northeast of Kontum.

The Binhar tribesmen quit their sorcerers and came

to her with their ailments after she stemmed an epidemic of a choleralike disease that frightened some of them into building their coffins. Her hospital—six one-story brick-and-cement buildings, staffed by Dr. Smith, four registered nurses, and five trained Montagnards—was tangible evidence of American friendship and peaceful purpose in Vietnam.

Many Americans believed that the key to victory in Vietnam lay in all Americans there helping the country with nation-building "civic action" that would win the goodwill of the inhabitants, as the work of Dr. Smith had done in Kontum. General Wallace M. Greene, Jr., the Marine commandant, spoke a much-quoted line about civic-action work. "If this effort fails," he said as his Leathernecks began a buildup around the port of Da Nang, "we could kill every Viet Cong and North Vietnamese in South Vietnam and still lose the war."

The Special Forces did their share of this work. From Kontum I was ordered to Saigon to attend a psychological-operations and civic-action school at Camp Goodman on Le Van Duyet Street. The capital was tense. There had been a riot led by Buddhist monks and nuns in front of the American Embassy protesting American support of the South Vietnam government. A mob of youths had smashed glass doors and windows in the U.S. Information Service library four blocks away.

"Don't let strangers get too close," a sergeant warned us. "One of them may drop a grenade in your pocket."

This was good advice. One of the greatest problems

in Vietnam is distinguishing friend from foe. Whether they are from the North or the South, Vietnamese look pretty much alike, speak and dress the same.

"If they salute, they're friendly," an old hand explained, "and if they shoot, they're not." It's too risky to wait to find out, and in the field it was the rule to consider everybody an enemy until a check-out proved otherwise. This caused trouble for some innocent people, but there was no other way to operate.

Air Marshal Nguyen Cao Ky, the pilot who became Premier of South Vietnam while I was serving there, was born in North Vietnam. He served in the French Army and fled to the South after the French defeat. Several of his generals also were from the North. Paradoxically, the Premier of North Vietnam, which was sending troops and arms South to help the Viet Cong fight the South Vietnam government and its American advisers, was Pham Van Dong, a man who had been born in South Vietnam.

Saigon is a fascinating place, and, except for landing and taking off from the airport, it was my first time there. It is a pretty city with a lot of French influence. All the barbers are French. They want to pluck your eyebrows and nostrils and clean out your ears for you. It is a very crowded city of many nationalities. Unless on official business, an American could hardly find a room. The U.S. Army had taken over several hotels, office buildings, and even a few night spots and made GI billets of them. More were being built, but in the meantime four to eight enlisted men were often crammed into one room.

Parts of Saigon are very American. Magazines like *Life, Reader's Digest, Time, Newsweek, Look,* and *Harper's* are on the newsstands almost as fast as back home. An edition of *Stars & Stripes* is flown in from Japan. The American Red Cross had a big office at Le Loi and Nguyen Hue Streets and smaller quarters elsewhere to help soldiers with their problems. There was an American-type bowling center on Nguyen Du Street.

There was an open-air black market offering nearly every kind of product, and those running it appeared to be prospering. But one local businessman had been condemned to death and publicly shot in Saigon's Central Market for "economic crime." The suicide rate was one of the highest in the world, partly because Buddhists believed they could attain nirvana by killing themselves as a form of political protest. But the leading method was neither fire nor firearms, despite all the guns around, but poison.

There were shortages of many things, even water. There was running water only in hotels and the more expensive housing areas. In the native quarters, water was available from central taps twice a day, and householders carried it away in cans slung over their shoulders. Telephone service was terrible. Electric power sometimes failed, halting elevators, water pumps, and air conditioning where it existed.

Traffic was insane. Some days it created more casualties than the war. You saw everything from Cadillacs to oxcarts, including a lot of bicycles and motor scooters, on the streets. Many natives new to the city would step directly in front of vehicles. As in New York, taxicabs were plentiful except during the rush hours and in rainstorms. Most soldiers got around the city via military buses, which ran every ten minutes or so.

Saigon long had French traffic cops, called "white mice" because of their uniforms. To free men for the war, the jobs were gradually being given to women. They looked very natty on duty in blue slacks, white shirts, little caps, and bright neck scarves. In fact, nearly all of the little, tiny-waisted, slim, delicate, serene Vietnamese women, either in uniform or out, were beautiful. Those I saw in the "Street of Flowers" were more attractive than the bright tropical blooms they were selling. High heels were part of everyday dress. Most wore the traditional *ao dai* costume, silk trousers and a silk overdress split down the sides. It is difficult for a GI even to meet a Vietnamese girl of good family, and the American military authorities do everything possible to discourage marriages with natives. For one thing, a soldier must submit sixteen documents, some in quintuplicate. But in 1965, at least sixty GI's found Vietnamese girls so irresistible that they married them in spite of all the red tape involved.

After the classes at Camp Goodman, we went partying and sight-seeing. "Night" spots along Tu Do Street open around 10 A.M. You have to fight your way sometimes through bar girls and begging children. To help part the soldier from his money, which was still dollars but which later became military scrip, many of the bars have names reminiscent of places back home. He can choose among the Hollywood, the Miami, the American, the Reno, the Princess, the Sporting Bar, and scores of others. One way or another, many bar girls earned the equivalent of several hundred dollars a month and a few lucky ones as much as a cabinet minister—that is, as somebody would always add, an "honest" cabinet minister.

Many of the children who wandered the streets were expert pickpockets, sometimes letting loose a balloon or doing something else to distract their victim's attention while they lifted his money.

Saigon shoeshine boys, who used to call Frenchmen "long noses," call Americans "big feet." While most local residents wouldn't think of paying more than five piasters for a shoeshine, Americans usually pay twenty, the equivalent of seventeen cents. "You number one!" shouts the shoeshine boy in thanks. If he has been paid less, he may yell, "You cheap Charlie—you number ten!" This is the ultimate insult.

Shotgun-armed Military Police, under the U.S. Navy except at the Tan Son Nhut air base, where the Air Force had the responsibility, helped enforce an 11 P.M. curfew in Saigon. After that, if you were in a hotel or apartment house, you often could go up on the roof and glimpse the flash of rockets and mortar fire in the distance and see searchlight-equipped helicopters seeking the Viet Cong in the nearby jungle.

The residents took it all in stride. Some had been at war for a long time, with the Japanese and the French before the Viet Cong and their North Vietnam supporters. The city seemed to view the war with a combination of courage, sangfroid, and fatalistic indifference. Some people organized "curfew" parties that began at midnight and ended at dawn. I never got there, but there was horse racing at the Saigon racetrack every weekend. Some restaurants, but only a few, put wire-mesh grills or adhesive tape over their windows to lessen possible bomb damage. Air-raid-shelter trenches, which had been dug in front of the Saigon city hall, actually were filled in and flowers planted there.

I later put my impressions of all this into a song with these words:

Saigon's a strange city
On the river Mekong shore,
A place that overnight
Makes a rich man poor,
A city where it's starve and feast,
The Paris of the East.
A young soldier far from home will sit down for a drink,
And a black-haired girl with almond eyes
Will help him not to think.
She'll play five hundred rummy for a drink or for love,
And you'll swear that she's an angel
That's come from up above.
Yes, then for a while life is good,
The night is sweet as honey,
Till the morning with bloodshot eyes

> You find you're out of money.
> So at Ton Son Nhut, you hop a plane
> And go back to the war.
> You've forgotten what it was you really came here for.
> Though you feel sick, your money is at an end,
> As you look down on old Saigon
> Think I'll be back again, I'll be back again.*

Saigon also has a more wholesome and happier side. There are schools, orphanages, and hospitals. For example, at the local U.S. Navy hospital, Lieutenant Commander Donald L. Kelley of Bellows Falls, Vermont, Captain Joseph W. Siegel of Hillside, New Jersey, and others have performed hairlip-correcting operations that have transformed the lives of more than a hundred Vietnamese children. When Vietnamese-government funds for the program were exhausted, U.S. Navy officers and men continued it with private contributions. Some Army hospitals in Vietnam have similarly aided cleft-palate victims.

Headquartered in Saigon are the vast Vietnam activities of the State Department's Agency for International Development (AID). This agency has spent millions improving agriculture and generally buttressing the South Vietnam economy. Some of its employees, Joseph W. Grainger of Meriden, Connecticut, for one, have been killed by the Viet Cong.

Through the U.S. Operations Mission, the AID has provided considerable medical assistance to the civilian population, refugees, and Vietnam military. When President Johnson, at the suggestion of Dr. Howard Rusk of New York, ordered fifty-six paraplegic Vietnamese soldiers airlifted from Saigon to the Veterans Administration Hospital at Castle Point, New York, the Operations Mission handled the job.

In a program sponsored by AID, the American Medical Association, and the People-to-People Health Foundation, scores of American doctors have gone to Vietnam to work without pay for two months or longer. These have included Dr. Malcolm Phelps of El Reno, Oklahoma; Dr. Richard E. Perry of St. Petersburg, Florida; Dr. Joseph Bryant of Lebanon, Tennessee; and Dr. Stephen Nagy of Baltimore, Maryland.

Our Special Forces civic-action course at Camp Goodman was a modest part of this big humanitarian program. We were told what help could be obtained from AID, the U.S. Operations Mission, the U.S. Information Service, and other sources. Successful local programs that might be applied elsewhere were described.

One team had revived the economy of a seaside village, by the production of Nuoc Mam, an odorous sauce made from fish that, like soy sauce, can be used on almost any food. Native troops in one camp were said to have refused to fight until they received their ration of Nuoc Mam.

Sergeant Gerald Grant, a medic with the First Special Forces "A" team, had set up a leper colony at Plei Mroung, a Montagnard village near Ban Me Thuot, the first ever organized by the Green Berets. By popularizing bathing, a deterrent to many other diseases besides leprosy, Grant lost only one patient in six months. With the help of Miss Ruth Whiting, a missionary at Ban Me Thuot, the leper colony became permanent, with some 460 lepers and their families living there.

It was near Plei Mroung that Sergeant Richard C. Ryan, one of my original teammates, was the hero of a bit of dramatic action. He was riding in the fourth truck back in a convoy ambushed by the Viet Cong. As he leaped over the side, he was shot in the elbow. Noticing that the engine of the truck was still running, he jumped back into it. With his good hand, he turned the truck out and around those ahead, literally running over three Viet Cong, and drove two miles into Plei Mroung, where he obtained help that routed the enemy.

At the end of the course at Camp Goodman, we received assignments. Both Lieutenant Jimmy Walker and I were assigned to Camp Hardy at Plei Do Lim, southeast of Pleiku. I had known Lieutenant Walker earlier at Fort Bragg. He was the son of Colonel Herman W. Walker of the Army, had been born in Fort Sill, Oklahoma, and had grown up in Gurdon, Arkansas. He had entered the Army via the Reserve Officers Training Corps at Henderson State Teachers College and had served with the 82nd Airborne before joining the Special Forces.

We took the commuter plane north together to Pleiku. He flew from there to Plei Do Lim, while I returned to Kontum to pick up my gear.

Life at Plei Do Lim

10 I FLEW thirty kilometers from Pleiku to Plei Do Lim in a few minutes by helicopter. The trip would have been a dangerous two hours by truck. There were then seventeen Special Forces camps in the Central Highlands. Most transportation between them was by Caribou aircraft and helicopters. The choppers were the real workhorses. They even airlifted cows. You couldn't give the people who make, fly, and service them enough praise. I was told it took four hours of maintenance for every hour in the air.

It was beautiful country, a plateau of lush grass with little patches of jungle, banana groves, and Montagnard villages all around. A sign on a roof identified rectangular Camp Hardy. It was named for Captain Herbert F. Hardy, Jr., of the First Special Forces, American commander at the camp a year earlier, who had been killed when his patrol was ambushed about two kilometers out of camp on March 4, 1964. The Special Forces demonstration area on Okinawa is also named for him.

Just before my helicopter landed on the adjoining airstrip, another one took off. Aboard, I learned, was Sergeant Kenneth Ellis, a Negro weapons man from Whiteville, North Carolina, who had been shot through the elbow in a clash with the Viet Cong. He had been one of three Americans accompanying a force of 144 Montagnard tribesmen from the camp on a patrol. He was evacuated to Pleiku and eventually to Womack Army Hospital at Fort Bragg, where he recovered and received the Purple Heart.

The first person I met was Captain Chandler P. Robbins III, commander of a Special Forces team—A-216, I believe. He was a slender third- or maybe a fourth-generation Army man from San Antonio, a cocky-looking little guy but a fine soldier and a very sharp man. He then had a mustache, but a few weeks later he had to shave it off when an order came down that everybody had to get rid of the handlebars. He had time only to show me my quarters in one of the underground bunkers, then the helicopters began to bring in the rest of the men who had been on patrol.

Leading them were Lieutenant Alfred Donovan Wilhelm, Jr., the team executive officer, who was from Little Rock, Arkansas, and Specialist Thor D. Johnson of Eureka, California, a demolition expert, a big guy of around six feet three inches and more than two hundred pounds, who had trained with me at Bragg. They looked tired and beat up. They had killed some VC and found a big cache of their guns. A remarkable thing about this ten-day patrol was that it had been staged during the New Year period, when practically all Vietnamese units stack arms and do not stir.

I met the other Americans in camp. There was, of course, Lieutenant Walker, who had arrived the day before. He later succeeded Lieutenant Wilhelm as executive officer when the latter was transferred to another Special Forces camp. Both later were promoted to captain. The team sergeant was Master Sergeant Francis Everett "Fritz" Manual from Bluemont, Virginia. He was in his middle forties, a well-built six-footer with graying hair. He later developed hepatitis and was evacuated out. In fact, he was in the hospital at Nha Trang when I was there. He was flown from there to Okinawa and finished his tour there.

The medics were Staff Sergeant Billy Johnson, a stocky, blond, blue-eyed man about my size, from Newtown, Missouri, and Staff Sergeant William LeGrand from Lima, Ohio, the same friendly fellow I had met in Hawaii who had said, "See you on Tu Do Street!" We never got there together, but I saw a lot of him.

Sergeants Philip Wayne Hunt and Patrick H. Holthusen were, respectively, senior and junior communications men. Both were very good. Hunt, who was from Firebaugh, California, had a touch of jungle rot in the feet that we were never able to clear up. Holthusen, from Chester, Arkansas, was a big six-foot kid of about twenty-three or twenty-four. The others were Sergeant First Class E. Sortillo, from Philadelphia; Staff Sergeant Billy Bean, a big fellow from Tennessee; and Staff Sergeant Fred J. Wright, the junior weapons man, another big fellow from the South, a fine professional soldier.

Billy Bean built the camp water tower, a fifty-five-gallon drum fifteen feet in the air that gave us showers when Montagnard muscles pumped it full of water. Billy also had the misfortune, as I've mentioned, to be bitten on the nose by a rat. He had to be rushed out for rabies shots. Billy was six feet three inches tall and weighed well over two hundred pounds. He was very quiet and said hardly anything. With the exception of Captain Robbins, Hunt, LeGrand, and myself, everybody on the team was big.

The South Vietnam flag flew over the camp and the commander was Captain Bui Van Lim of the South Vietnamese Special Forces (called the LLDB for short; the letters stand for Luc-Luong Dac-Biet). Captain Lim was from North Vietnam and had fought with the Nationalist forces against the French. Not caring for the Communists, who took over the movement, he came south.

In addition to Captain Lim, there were six to eight other LLDB men in camp being trained and advised by their American counterparts. Then there were three hundred or so Montagnards organized as a strike force. Until a few days earlier, the camp had included some Chinese Nungs, valuable but troublesome mercenaries. Some Nungs had been in Vietnam a long time.

Several thousand more had fled south when the Communists took over China. When Vietnam was partitioned, they moved again to South Vietnam. For a time, they composed a division of the South Vietnamese Army and sometimes charged into battle with smoking sticks of incense tied to their weapons. President Ngo Dinh Diem, however, feared this force of four thousand Nungs and before his assassination scattered them among many units. This made for friction. While they usually got along very well with Americans (some GI's actually paid out of their own pockets to have them around as personal bodyguards), the Nungs were scornful of all other troops. In addition, they were paid the equivalent of $8 more a month than our Montagnards.

It was cheating at cards, however, that caused the

Nungs to be thrown out of Plei Do Lim. But they were not lost to the war effort. With Nungs from other camps, they were organized later at Pleiku into a "Mike" force that was rushed by air to the aid of any camp in the area that the Viet Cong threatened to overrun. They fought well at Plei Me, twenty miles southwest of Plei Do Lim, where a Special Forces team watched for infiltrators from the west.

The mission of Camp Hardy was to protect the ten thousand Montagnards in Plei Do Lim and the surrounding villages from the Viet Cong, who earlier had burned some of the settlements, and by good works to win their loyalty to the government. The authorities had not carried out the promises made to the Montagnards after their revolt, and there were continual rumors of new revolts. It was our job to advise, to lead, to instruct these people, to give them the benefit of our guidance, what we knew.

With all the languages involved, interpreters were very important. A very sharp man named Lee was the senior interpreter. We had a Montagnard named Henry who spoke English, Vietnamese, and two Montagnard dialects. We had a Chinese, Fong, who worked as a cook until he learned enough English to interpret. Later we hired Chan, a nineteen-year-old boy from Saigon, to interpret between the LLDB and us. He was a favorite of mine.

A small Montagnard medic with a harelip, known as "little *bac-si*," had been the hero of the patrol that had brought in the weapons. The arms had been protected by a Viet Cong minefield with a lot of signs in Vietnamese warning people away. The Montagnard volunteered, went in, and passed the more than fifty guns out. These weapons were a lethal hodgepodge. There were some American carbines, a couple of Springfield rifles, some shotguns, a British Mark I Lee Enfield, some French light machine guns, and many other French weapons. Several of these bore the markings of French Mobile Group 100, which was an armored force, composed of some of the finest French troops, that had been almost wiped out in the area in 1954 while the attention of the world was focused on the fall of Dienbienphu in northern Vietnam. After more than a decade, weapons, uniforms, overcoats, and other items bearing the regimental stampings of the ill-fated unit still could be found among the local tribesmen, and the rusted hulks of its vehicles were encountered along Highways 14 and 19.

The haul brought praise for the camp from General Harold K. Johnson, the Army chief of staff, who wrote General Westmoreland to "pass to these fine American soldiers my heartiest commendations for their actions, which reflected great credit upon the U.S. Army."

One of the many odd things about the war in Vietnam is that it sometimes stops for holidays. It came to a halt during the first week of February, when the natives celebrated the lunar New Year as the Year of the Dragon ended and the Year of the Snake began. Vietnamese TET, as the lunar New Year is called, is really a combination of Christmas and All Souls' Day. It is a time when families like to be together if at all possible. Both the government and the Viet Cong made great propaganda efforts during this season urging the many divided families to unite in their support. There were special leaflets, special songs, special radio appeals.

Over their radio, the Communists announced a seven-day cease-fire. Two hours after it ended, on February 7, they made a terrific attack on Camp Holloway in Pleiku. It was a very clear night, and from Camp Hardy we could see planes dropping flares, lighting the sky, and the flames of burning aircraft. One party of Viet Cong raiders cut through the barbed wire around the airfield to blow up twenty aircraft with satchel charges. Another group opened up with mortars on a compound where 400 Americans slept. A third group attacked corps headquarters, where 180 others were billeted.

A sentry, Jesse Pyle of Marina, California, was killed as he gave the alarm at headquarters, and seven other Americans lost their lives. Their bodies were flown to the United States in flag-draped caskets. There were 109 wounded, 76 seriously enough for evacuation. It was strictly an attack on Americans. There were no casualties at all among the 4,300 Vietnamese in Pleiku that night. Papers found on bodies of the slain Viet Cong showed that the attack had been planned in North Vietnam. The war became grimmer.

Our planes, until then restricted to a few retaliatory strikes in the North, began systematic bombing north of the 17th parallel, both with explosives and with propaganda. Families of American soldiers and civilians in South Vietnam were ordered out of the country. Most of the eighteen hundred dependents returned to the United States. General Westmoreland's family went to Hawaii, and more than a hundred families moved to Bangkok in nearby Thailand. Several hundred single American women employed by the U.S. Embassy in Saigon, the U.S. Information Service, the AID, the United Service Organizations, and other government and private agencies continued at their jobs.

Camp Hardy was a model of security. A great deal of thought had been given to preventing any sort of surprise like that at Pleiku. Ours was a strong camp, very well set up, with many defenses. We worked on them continually, frequently changing things. In fact, the only successful invaders were insects. We once had a three-day invasion of termites. They came by the thousand, all over everything, in the food, in your hair. Another time a swarm of bees blew through the camp.

We had inner- and outer-perimeter defenses. The outer perimeter had only one entrance, with all kinds of weapons trained on it. There were underground bunkers, individual foxholes, and numerous fortifications and positions connected by a trench running around the edge of the camp. Sandbags topped with barbed wire formed another perimeter. There were ditches lined with *punji* sticks and claymore mines. A claymore mine, which is named for the two-edged claymore sword once used by Scottish Highlanders for close fighting, weighs only two and a half pounds but sprays about seven hundred deadly steel fragments in a fan-shaped zone. It can be fired electrically or by three pounds of pull or eight pounds of pressure. It is an American development, but the Viet Cong have one too.

At least one American was awake all night. It was his job to go along with one of his Montagnards to inspect the perimeter at least once an hour, checking that all guards were awake, weapons in place and working. We had an electrical alarm system connected to the barbed wire, as well as three separate electric generators and a fortified watchtower forty-five feet high with searchlights sweeping the perimeter. Sentries were up there day and night.

Our greatest strength came, however, from our good relations with the Montagnards and from our patrols. When the Viet Cong entered or approached the nearby villages, our friends gave us warning. This had not happened at Pleiku. We always had at least one patrol out. Each patrol ordinarily lasted a week and usually consisted of one or two Americans, one or two members of the Vietnamese Special Forces, and twelve to one hundred Montagnards. Nearly everybody wore jungle-camouflage suits.

Sergeant Wright took me out on my first patrol, a search-and-destroy operation, a week or so after my arrival. We had been out only a day, when a rumor reached the camp that the Viet Cong were planning to attack it. We made a forced march of fifteen miles to get back close to Plei Do Lim, only to be told that the report had proved false and that we were to resume the patrol. I was panting and wheezing.

Our orders sent us east to the Ayun River. I then went north, and Sergeant Wright went south. Each of us had about fifty Montagnards with us. We had no VC contacts that day. That night we camped on a mountainside overlooking a waterfall on a known VC route.

We picked up a couple of suspected Viet Cong, a young man and an older man who said the younger man was his son. The older man later admitted to being a VC who had been "retired" or "relieved" because of his age. He proved to be a source of intelligence, and we kept him with us for the rest of the patrol.

We sat up there that night and placed outposts and little ambushes along trails that the Viet Cong might travel. Around 11 P.M. or midnight, one of my men thought he saw somebody trying to come up the hill through the jungle. Something did seem to be moving, and I took a shot. I think I killed a tree. For the rest of the night it was quiet.

In the morning, we made radio contact again with camp and proceeded down the river to a rendezvous with Sergeant Wright. On the way we ran into a cache of about a thousand kilos of rice, which we burned. In the villages, we asked about the Viet Cong, whether they had come through or had been active. Most villagers were too scared to say much. Young men were absent in all these villages, a sure sign that the Viet Cong had been there recruiting and had taken them away.

We blasted up some fish from the river with grenades and a pinch of TNT. Some of the troops dived in and got some nice carp, which we roasted to mix with our rice. On a patrol, we usually took one wet ration and cooked only once a day. Whatever we came across on the trail went into the pot. We frequently ate a mixture of C rations, stewed fish, and boiled ants. Villagers sometimes sold or traded us chickens. Even if they didn't want to sell and we took them, we paid.

With the whole patrol reunited, we crossed the Ayun River into definitely Viet Cong territory, sending out points and flankers to avoid any ambushes or surprises. There was none. We tramped about a bit, burned some fields, and returned. It was just a search, something to keep the VC aware that we were there. By the end of the patrol, we had six suspects, and two of them turned out to be Viet Cong. They were questioned and sent to the Vietnamese Special Forces headquarters at Pleiku.

On many patrols, I would have a sort of sick call, especially for the children, in the villages that we visited. I found considerable satisfaction in this. They often asked me to leave medicine so that they could continue treatment. We couldn't do that, since anything we left would be confiscated by the VC. But we told the patients and their families that if they came to Plei Do Lim, they would be treated. Many did so.

With a dozen Americans rotating the patrols, each drew a week-long one only every six weeks. This left a lot of time for other activities, even for rest and recreation. We were allowed one in-country and one out-of-country "R and R" of ten days each, at places like Nha Trang, Saigon,

Bangkok, and Hong Kong. When the convoys were running, it was easy to get up to Pleiku.

Everybody observed *Pak*, or siesta time, from about 11 A.M. to 1 P.M. or later. Noel Coward wrote his famous song "Mad Dogs and Englishmen" while driving across what is now Vietnam. Everything he said about the folly of going "out in the midday sun" was true. It was so hot during the day and we slept so poorly at night, what with the rats and other small animals, that we really needed our naps. My narrow underground bunk, in which the logs were still sprouting greenery, was musty and moldy but was about the coolest spot in camp.

Our communications people and some others listened regularly to Australian radio broadcasts. Because of some peculiarities of the mountains, it was hard to pick up Saigon and Hanoi. The stations easiest to pick up, strangely enough, were Radio Moscow and Radio Armenia, also in Soviet Russia. They were loud and clear, but they didn't seem to have in mind young Green Berets in the highlands when planning programs. Since then an Armed Forces television network has been started in Vietnam.

Captain Robbins and some of us played cards every night in the team room. There was an 11 P.M. curfew on the game except for the rare times that Captain Robbins was winning. "I'm running this blankity-blank camp," he'd then announce. "It's no longer eleven o'clock—it's now eight o'clock. Deal."

We played poker, blackjack, acey-deucey, high-low, all the stud games, just about everything. But poker was

the most popular. The most consistent winners were Lieutenant Walker, Fred Wright, and myself. After Sergeant
Wright was shifted to a camp up near Da Nang on the
coast, Lieutenant Walker and I sort of lost interest.

Before he left, Wright asked me to teach him to play
the guitar. He learned just one piece, "Tom Dooley," before shipping out. We heard that old ballad over and over
for three months.

I played my guitar a bit too and wrote two more
songs. One of them was inspired by a Bill Mauldin cartoon.
Besides appearing in the Chicago *Sun-Times* and other
dailies, his cartoons are seen by soldiers in the *Army
Times*. Mauldin was a sergeant in World War II and
came out to Vietnam to see his son, Bruce, an Army
helicopter pilot at Pleiku. He also visited Camp Hardy.
What caught my eye was Mauldin's drawing of a corpulent
garrison trooper decked out with every imaginable acces-
sory and even wearing brass-plated bullets. The idea was
underlined when I saw a dapper, similarly accoutered
young Vietnamese pilot crash an L-19 spotter aircraft on
our airstrip and walk away, his pistol and bandoliers clink-
ing, saying, "Oh, well, they'll give me another one." My
friend Sergeant Sortillo also suggested some points. I
called the song "Garet Trooper." The lines, some to be
spoken, are:

> Now, in the war-torn jungles of Vietnam,
> You'll find a certain kind of man,
> You'll see him everywhere.

He's a trooper . . . a Garet trooper.
Yah, he's five foot four,
Two hundred and twenty-eight pounds of blubber.
Got him a nickel-plated forty-five,
Tied-down-low quick-draw holster,
Two bandoliers of brasso-ed ammo. . . .
He's fought from Saigon to Nha Trang,
In every bar that is, and then only with the girls,
And he ain't won one yet. . . .
He's got a hip knife, a side knife, a boot knife,
A shoulder knife, and a little bitty one,
A combination flare gun, dinner set,
Genuine police whistle. . . .*

The other song was inspired by some correspondence
with my wife, Lavona. She wrote that she was playing
tapes of my songs to our son, Thor. To see that he had
everything, she was working at not one but two jobs in
Lehighton. She got up at 5 A.M., took care of Thor, and
worked from 7 A.M. to 3:30 P.M. at a rug mill mending
carpets. She then worked from 4 P.M. to midnight as a
waitress at the Big Chief drive-in restaurant in Packerton,
near Jim Thorpe. When I heard about this, I had a fit
and made her give up the second job. Soon after this, I
wrote a song titled "Letter from Vietnam":

Oh, Lord, I'm tired and sad,
And I want you, oh, so bad.

> I've been away so very long;
> Now I want to go home.
> So remember that I love you;
> That, my dear, is true.
> Just say a prayer for your man—
> This letter's postmarked Vietnam.
> Last night we had a fire fight,
> Machine guns firing tracers through the night,
> And as we fought, my thoughts,
> They turned to you.
> And I knew somehow, darling,
> I'll come through. . . .*

Instead of writing Lavona a letter, I sent her a tape of this song.

* Copyright © 1965 and 1966 by Music Music Music Inc.

Civic Action

11 THE "A" TEAM at Camp Hardy already had two medics, Sergeants LeGrand and Johnson, when I arrived. There were few casualties, and nearly everybody was in good health. So I first had the assignment of being a psychological-warfare civic-action sergeant, a role not defined exactly in the Special Forces organization charts.

As part of this job, a newly arrived lieutenant decided that I should go into brickmaking. He gave me a little hand machine that pressed one brick at a time out of whatever you put into it. The idea was for us to develop something that the tribesmen could use to build better houses than their miserable thatched hovels. My job was to find the right combination of the available ingredients to make a good brick. A good brick is not supposed to dissolve in water or crumble. It also is supposed to be firm and strong.

I bet I made ten thousand of those overgrown mud pies. Some were so hard you couldn't break them with a hammer, but if a drop of water touched them they would disintegrate. Others you could put in the shower without harm, but hit them with a piece of paper and they would fall apart.

After five or six weeks, I seemed to have the answer. It was an adobe-type brick made from red clay, mud, straw, grass, and lime. A shower bath didn't hurt it. I jumped up and down on it in my paratrooper boots and couldn't dent it. I took it into the captain's office and gave him a smart salute. "Sir," I announced, "I finally got my brick. This is it."

I dropped it on his desk and the brick broke in two. This was the end of the brick project.

"Sadler," somebody asked afterward, "what are you going to tell your kid you did in Vietnam?"

"That I made mud pies," I answered.

Some other civic-action projects were more successful. For one thing, my friend Sergeant LeGrand got tired of his medic assignment, and we gradually exchanged jobs. I was then a junior medic, Specialist-5. I began to spend more and more time in the dispensary, and he took over a lot of the civic action, though everybody in camp was involved in it in one way or another.

LeGrand built a great big chicken coop in Chief Do Khac Hoan's village. It was the best structure there. It was so much better than the chief's house that we thought he might chase the chickens out and move in himself. Chief Hoan, a very fine man, was an important ally of Camp Hardy. He was a subsector leader and the top civilian in the neighborhood, a Vietnamese who lived with the Montagnards. He had armed a little force of his own with carbines and Thompson submachine guns to protect his village, which was just a kilometer from our camp. Anytime Chief Hoan had any news, he called us over a radiophone set we had given him. His news was sometimes very important.

Besides showing the tribesmen how to raise chickens better, we helped them with their pigs and crops. Through the AID program, they could obtain farm implements, seed, chemical fertilizers, and even schoolhouses and school books if somebody showed them how to go about it. We did so well on the food front that our Montagnards, mostly of the Djari and Bihnar tribes, were healthier than those in the backlands. Even photographs showed the difference.

We encouraged the villagers to make articles that they could sell. The women in our area made small houses that were shipped to Kontum, where they sold readily for four dollars each to helicopter pilots and others. This would feed a family for a week or two. Our villagers also developed a business in souvenir spears and crossbows. The full-size crossbow is a powerful weapon that can put an arrow through a banana tree. Marine Sergeant Glenn C. Bagerstock and several Americans have been wounded by them in Vietnam. Toy crossbows are great for shooting rats, and we made a sport of this in the underground bunkers of Camp Hardy.

A chaplain, Lieutenant Colonel Carl P. McNally from Fayetteville, North Carolina, helped the Koho tribe of Montagnards in a similar crossbow enterprise at Da Me, forty kilometers south of Dalat. He shipped their crossbows, spears, and handwoven blankets to Saigon for sale to soldiers. Purchases brought in more than $10,000, which the village used to buy food, medicine, lumber, and a tractor, as well as to help build a new church.

Special Forces men were so successful at this sort of thing that many of them wound up working for AID in one way or another. Lieutenant Colonel Harry H. Jackson, Jr., a University of Michigan graduate, for example, was picked for special detached service in this program and became a regional director in the vital Mekong Delta area, where forty percent of the population live. After leaving the Green Berets, George Gaspard became Quang Duc Province director for the agency.

There were more Americans working for AID in Vietnam in 1965 than in any of its seventy-one other missions around the world. In the previous five years, the agency had helped to erect in South Vietnam 4,682 new classrooms, drilled 1,900 freshwater wells, constructed 12,000 village health clinics, and doubled the production of pigs. It had given out eight million textbooks to schoolchildren. These were written by Vietnamese educators and printed under AID auspices, mostly in Manila and Hong Kong.

With only nine hundred Vietnamese physicians to treat a population of sixteen million, medical aid was the most welcome. Billy Johnson and I did all we could in this direction. Without any warning or prior notification, we would hop into a truck and run sick calls in a few villages. If we had given any notice or had attempted to maintain a regular schedule or route, we probably would have been murdered by the Viet Cong.

"*Bac-si! Bac-si!*" Somebody would call as we arrived. Mothers would bring out their children. The ill would gather, and we soon had all the patients we could handle. We treated a lot of trachoma, the eye disease. Somebody estimated that four-fifths of the population had it. A little application of antibiotics worked wonders in most cases. We'd put patients who were crippled or seriously ill in the truck and bring them back to camp. We kept some for weeks, feeding and treating them.

Other Special Forces camps did the same thing. Down in Chaudoc Province, Sergeants George Decker and Joe Brock of Captain John F. Conlon's "A" team fitted up a "deuce and a half," an Army two-and-a-half-ton truck, as a rolling dispensary. They got around to thirty villages and hamlets with a total population of eighty thousand. Up in Khesonh, near both the Laos border and the demilitarized zone, Sergeant Thomas O'Leary from Hampden, Maine, took along on such visits two Vietnamese girls he had trained as nurses. We had a Vietnamese nurse named Marie with us part of the time at Camp Hardy. She was too tiny and excitable to take out on patrols, but we let her pull teeth in the dispensary.

Camp Hardy was known for its excellent relations with the Montagnards as well as for its security. We all wore the thin brass Montagnard brotherhood bracelets. We had no caste system and mingled more freely with the tribesmen than most American soldiers did in other places. We built them a little post exchange in camp where they could buy beer and other Vietnam goods. After a successful fight or patrol, we would have a party down there. They had gongs, and I brought my guitar. I'd sing; they'd sing. They sang in Bihnar, telling what good soldiers they were, how they had fought the Viet Cong, and what had happened. We would harmonize. I didn't know what they were singing and vice versa, but everybody had a good time. Everybody except those on duty would get three-quarters lit and then go to bed.

When an American Broadcasting Company crew shot a film on the Montagnards, a Public Information Officer brought the cameramen and others from Saigon to Camp Hardy. We arranged the sacrifice of a water buffalo with full native ceremony for the visitors. Men, women, and children came from the surrounding Montagnard villages for this.

The water buffalo was brought in suspended by his hooves from a long pole. A shaman, or witch doctor, appeared. The women and children beat gongs with strips of wood and bamboo. The tempo was slow. Women danced around in a little two-step shuffle, left-right, left-right, back one, all linking hands. The men danced around them in a larger circle. This went on for quite a while.

Then the shaman came out, sprinkled rice powder to the four winds, and began to chant. This was supposed to frighten off evil spirits and to purify the water buffalo. He then called out a prominent villager, in this case Hmau, one of the Montagnard company commanders, to do the sacrificing.

Hmau immobilized the buffalo by cutting its leg tendons with a small hatchet and then killed the animal with several thrusts of a spear. As soon as the buffalo was dead, it was rolled, without any skinning or gutting, onto a fire of wood and bamboo. Twenty minutes later, the participants began to cut off chunks of meat and eat them. A variety of native intoxicants washed them down. Everybody slept late the next morning.

We had a number of visitors at the camp. Besides cartoonist Bill Mauldin, there were Jack Langguth of *The New York Times*, Chuck Keen of Alaska Pictures, Jim Lucas of the Scripps-Howard newspapers, Peter Lisagor of the Chicago *News*, Slam Marshall of the Detroit *News*, Chesly Manly of the Chicago *Tribune*, and others. Harold H. Martin from Atlanta visited his son, John, a soldier in the 1st Cavalry Division over at An Khe, and wrote a *Saturday Evening Post* article about it.

Soldiers don't like to have visitors on patrols and in places of great danger. Dickey Chapelle, a woman writer for *Reader's Digest*, was killed while visiting a dangerous area. So was Sam Castan, an editor of *Look*, ironically just after saying that he wanted to learn "the thoughts of men facing death."

In hospitals and safe areas, it's a different story. The more visitors, especially if they are entertaining, the better. Martha Raye visited the Eighth Field Hospital at Nha Trang when I was a patient there and made a big hit with everybody. She is quite a woman and works hard. She made two long tours of Vietnam posts, often wearing a "tiger" camouflage suit. Out at Bac Lieu, a bunker is named Fort Martha Raye.

Mary Martin, Danny Kaye, John Wayne, George Jessel, Edgar Bergen, and many other show people made at least brief visits. So did Hugh O'Brian, who on his return home telephoned, in many cases long distance, relatives of Green Berets he had visited in camp. This was a pleasant surprise for many mothers and wives. In fact, one girl fell off her chair. Bob Hope, Raymond Burr, Roy Acuff, Eddie Fisher, Kathy Nolan, Frances Langford, Charlton Heston, Robert Mitchum, and Roy Rogers also visited Vietnam.

Among the visitors were less well-known pretty girls like Leigh Ann Austin, Miss Texas of 1961, and Chanin Hale of *The Red Skelton Show*, who brightened our days. When a company of the 173rd Airborne Brigade at Bien Hoa sent a lifetime subscription to *Playboy* with a letter saying "loneliness here is a terrible thing—and we long to see a real, living, breathing American girl," the magazine flew over its Playmate of the Year, Jo Collins, from Seattle and Hollywood, to deliver the first copy. She also visited Special Forces camps at the Black Virgin Mountain, Lay Ninthe, and Bu Dop. There one of my Bragg buddies, Sergeant Art Golden of Youngstown, Ohio, was photographed with her. It made his day.

Lightning and Leaflets

12 AN OTTER airplane swooped down on Camp Hardy one morning in March when I was working on the machine-gun bunker. After running the daily sick call, there was usually time before lunch to do another job—build something new, lay in more barbed wire, sharpen *punji* sticks, or train troops. That morning I was wearing dirty old fatigues and I had red clay all over me.

"Sergeant Sadler," called the pilot, "get ready to move out!"

I grabbed my machine gun, an AR-15 about which I later sang a song, and my gear. The little plane circled and landed on the airstrip, and I climbed aboard.

"Where am I going?" I asked.

"Saigon," answered the pilot.

"What for?"

"I don't know. I just have orders to deliver you to Saigon."

Cruddy, filthy, and needing a shave, I got off the plane carrying my AR-15. There was nobody to meet me, and I didn't know where to go. Eventually somebody remembered that an Army Public Information Officer, a major, was looking for me. I remembered him as PIO with the cameramen who had filmed our Montagnards. At that time he had said something about asking me to help him sometime.

I never knew there were so many PIO's in Saigon. I had to go through at least ten of them before finding the right one. PIO's don't lead an easy life. They are not Garet

147

troopers but frequently are much harassed men who have to deal with all manner of odd problems, with little chance of keeping everybody happy. I knew one once who was in trouble with his superiors for getting too much notice for his outfit, but every man in it thought it wasn't getting enough.

When I found the major, he told me he had two projects. He wanted to film and tape me singing "The Ballad" for television. He also, and more urgently, wanted me to compose a song in honor of Major General Delk N. Oden, the Flying General, who was head of the Army Support Command in Vietnam. General Oden had a big and unique job. Under him were all the Special Forces units and all the aviation battalions. Since 1961, the command had grown from a few troops to more than ten thousand. Its job was to keep the aviation units flying, the communications working, the traffic flowing, the troops supplied with ammunition, food, and clothing, and their health taken care of by field hospitals and medical detachments.

General Oden was from Elgin, Texas, and had graduated from West Point in 1937. He was then a horse cavalryman and in World War II a tank commander under General Patton in Europe. Oden had won the Distinguished Service Cross and the Bronze Star for Valor and had served all over—Scofield Barracks, Hawaii; Fort Bliss, Texas; Fort Riley, Kansas; Pine Camp, New York. He had been military attaché in Vienna and director of the Turkish Armored School in Ankara.

When a colonel and more than forty-six years old, he

learned to fly at Fort Rucker, Alabama, and continued to do so. He was perhaps the only officer of his rank actually to pilot aircraft in Vietnam at the time. This was why he was called the Flying General. He took the same risks as his men and often flew his own helicopter on airlifts to the battle zone, once landing it in a town still held by the Viet Cong to help carry out some wounded.

He was proud of his men and quick to praise them. After a brush with the Viet Cong near Ca Mau, he authorized on the spot the award of thirty-two Air Medals for Valor to two helicopter companies that had distinguished themselves in the action. Things like this made him popular. So when the word came that he was shipping out to another job in Washington, D.C., his officers undertook to give him a memorable farewell party. This was where I came into the picture.

"Okay, sir," I said, and went to work.

It was no trouble. As my friend Robert Macdonald, El Flaco of Sam Houston and Bragg, often said, I write songs "like a hydrant." In a few minutes I had something, a sort of ode to Oden, with lines about fighting and flying. The major was very happy and insisted that I sing the song at the party. I agreed. In the meantime he borrowed some clean clothes and a guitar for me and showed me some rather handsome hospitality.

I was still feeling and showing the effects of this when I showed up the party next day. The place was surrounded by barbed wire and fortified like Fort Knox. Two big MP's armed with shotguns stood guard at the gate.

"Where do you think you are going?" demanded one.

"I'm going to play my guitar for the general," I replied.

"Man," he said, "you are stupid. Go on, get out of here."

"But I want to play my guitar for the general."

"Quit bugging me. Run along, now."

We were just about to get into a fight, when the major came and got me and took me inside.

I never such an array of stars, eagles, and medals of all kinds. Besides General Oden, there were his successor, Major General John Norton, and maybe a dozen other generals. General Norton was another Texan, from the little town of Round Rock. He was a 1941 graduate of West Point, had served at Bragg and in Europe during World War II with the 82nd Airborne, and had fought in Korea. He later commanded the 1st Air Cavalry Division in Vietnam.

Somebody knocked on a glass, the noise quieted down, and I sang and played the song for the Flying General. I forgot about half the lines and had to ad-lib as I went along. Nobody knew the difference, and I got a big hand.

There were a lot of Special Forces officers present. "'The Green Beret,'" somebody shouted. "Sing 'The Green Beret.'"

I looked over all the insignia and laughed. "Since I'm the lowest-ranking so-and-so here," I said, "I guess I'd better."

We gave General Oden a tape of my singing at the party. He thanked us and put it into a box with his flag and medals for shipment to the States. There was the threat of a strike or something, and next day he flew out on a military plane to the Philippines instead of taking a Pan American airliner. He arrived safely in Washington, D.C., to become director of officer personnel in the Army's Office of Personnel Operations, but the box containing the tape was never seen again. I didn't keep a copy or a tape and have been unable to recall either the words or the music. Unless the PIO people saved a tape, the song is lost forever.

Next day the PIO major had me sing "The Ballad" standing in front of a bunker in Saigon. An American Broadcasting Company team filmed and recorded me for television back home. I then took one of the C-130 shuttle planes up to Pleiku, with a stop at Ban Me Thuot en route, and a chopper from Pleiku to Plei Do Lim.

Something horrible had happened at Camp Hardy on the afternoon of March 27, a Saturday, while I had been singing in Saigon. I had certainly been lucky that day.

Medic Billy Johnson had been playing pinochle in our underground dispensary and looking out the window now and then at the rain coming down. Suddenly he noticed a great flash of blazing white light, then—*blam! blam!*—two thunderous explosions.

Sergeant Hunt, the communications man, thought it was a mortar attack. He grabbed his microphone and into it yelled, "Stand by, stand by!"

Screams, some from women and children, and cries of "Help, *bac-si!*" rose from several directons. Billy Johnson and others rushed out from their shelters.

It took a few minutes to discover what had happened. A bolt of lightning had struck near the barbed wire, exploding thirty-six of eighty-four claymore mines in an irregular pattern around the entire perimeter. The deadly metal pellets had torn through buildings, vehicles, and people.

Ninety-three persons had been killed or injured in the fraction of a second. Thirty of those hit died, fourteen at once and the others days or weeks later. A Vietnamese woman cook and six prisoners, suspected Viet Cong who had been carrying wood at the time of the blast, were among the dead.

When he found that it was not a mortar attack, Sergeant Hunt called in doctors and helicopters from Pleiku. Over his radio he heard the "scramble" and "dust-off" commands there. A few minutes later the choppers began to arrive and take away the seriously wounded. Those who survived were later returned to Plei Do Lim, and I helped treat them.

Lieutenant Walker had been in Pleiku at the time of the blast and returned to camp on one of the rescue helicopters. With one exception, all Americans in the camp were either away or underground or behind the exploding claymore mines, which had been aimed outward from the inner perimeter. The unlucky exception was my friend Sergeant Bill LeGrand from Ohio. He was entering the LLDB mess hall, between the inner and outer perimeters, when the lightning struck. Steel pellets from the detonated claymores caught him in the head and stomach. He was gravely injured and evacuated first to Pleiku, then to Nha Trang, then to Saigon, and next to Clark Air Force Hospital in the Philippines.

Both Bill and his wife, Beverly, had had eerie premonitions that he would not return from Vietnam. That was why he had been flying home on emergency leave when I met him in Hawaii. "I think he felt he had to come home for Christmas, because of me, for the last time," explained Mrs. LeGrand later. "We both had taken the death of our baby son badly and were homesick for each other. In some of his last letters, he wrote 'if I make it.' He never wrote 'if' in any of his letters before December.

"When I saw the boy on the bicycle looking at addresses along the street, I knew the telegram was about Bill even before I received it."

The Army flew Beverly out to Bill in Clark Air Force Hospital. Though he had just had a third operation and, because of pneumonia, was breathing through an opening cut in his neck, he greeted her cheerfully and asked about their daughters.

A kidney specialist was flown in from Japan, and three days later Bill and Beverly were flown to the Tachikawa hospital in Japan. There he had a fourth operation and was treated with the latest respirators and kidney machines. He fought hard to live, and the doctors did everything possible. It was all in vain. He died on April 28, the same date that he had joined the Army fifteen years earlier. Beverly was with him. He is buried in Ada, Ohio, where he had been Army adviser to the National Guard and where he had met Beverly.

Bill was given a Bronze Star and the Purple Heart. A twenty-one-year-old Marine, John Edgerly of Grand Rapids, Michigan, who was killed by lightning while on sentry duty near Da Nang, however, was refused the latter on the ground that his injuries were not the result of enemy action. At his funeral back in Michigan, Tom Klein, a friend of Edgerly and former Marine who had lost a leg after stepping on a Viet Cong mine, took off his own Purple Heart and pinned it on the pillow in Edgerly's casket.

"I figure anyone who has guts enough to fight over there, no matter how he dies, deserves recognition," said Klein at the time. I agree with this, and so do the Vietnamese. They decorated nearly every American who died there. If he was killed in action, he received both their Military Merit Medal and their Military Gallantry Cross for Valor. Congress passed a law in 1965 authorizing American soldiers to wear decorations awarded them by Vietnam and the nations allied with us there.

Tom Klein, incidentally, received another Purple Heart to replace the one buried with Edgerly. When Klein's friends reported his action to President Johnson, the President ordered another sent. "I am proud to join them," the President wrote him, "in saluting not only your courage but your compassion. . . . I believe you have helped advance the day when all men will care for their fellows as deeply as you did for John Edgerly."

We never did receive a replacement for Sergeant Le-Grand at Camp Hardy. In fact, it would have been hard to find another man so generous, so friendly, so brave.

Three days after I left Saigon, the Viet Cong exploded a dynamite bomb in front of the American Embassy there. By then I was back, of course, at Plei Do Lim, where, that day at least, things were peaceful. I began to believe that I had been born under a lucky star. Twenty-two persons, including two Americans, were killed, and one hundred and ninety were hurt. The Americans killed were Barbara Robbins, a twenty-one-year-old stenographer from Denver, and Navy storekeeper Manolito W. Castillo, an Embassy clerk.

The dynamite, hidden in a small Renault automobile, shattered all the windows in the front of the five-story Embassy and blew the glass inward. Miss Robbins died at her desk holding a ball-point pen. When the bombed facade was replaced, the walls were made thicker and the size of the windows cut down. Barbed wire and concrete blocks were added in front.

President Johnson made a speech in Baltimore on April 17 promising that the independence of South Vietnam would be preserved but offering to take part in unconditional peace discussions. His words triggered an escalation of the propaganda side of the war. Leaflets bearing the President's picture and portions of his Baltimore speech, translated into Vietnamese and other languages, were dropped by our planes over both North and South Vietnam.

That month the Joint U.S. Public Affairs Office was set up in Saigon to coordinate and direct all American psychological activities in the country. Some of those involved still were trying to avoid use of the word "war." Staffing JUSPAO were 400 Vietnamese and 150 Americans, some military and some civilians. The director was Armenian-born Barry Zorthian of the U.S. Information Service. Zorthian had been a field-artillery officer with the 1st Marine Division in World War II and later a Columbia Broadcasting System news editor. One of the deputies was General Freund, who had helped quell the Montagnard rebellion.

Soon our planes were dropping millions of leaflets every day that they flew. Some were "surrender passes," similar in words and format to those of World Wars I and II, promising defectors that they would be well treated and telling them where and how to give up. Others promised bombings and warned recipients away from military targets. Many were letters from defectors. Some were copies of an airborne newspaper called *Nhan Van*, translated as both "Human Knowledge" and "True News." A few had beautiful slick-paper color-printing formats. Most were simple, cartoon-illustrated documents, appropriate for a region where the level of literacy is low.

Some of the leaflets fluttered unseen into the jungle or sea, but many were dropped accurately by low-flying armored helicopters whose loudspeakers urged people to pick them up. Some fell to the third of the population who cannot read. (Some of our tribesmen couldn't even count.)

Many leaflets reached those who could read but could not act. But the expense was trifling in comparison with other costs of the war, and the operation was considered worthwhile.

Leaflets were an important factor in luring more than thirty-six thousand persons from the North to the South side of the struggle in the operation called *Chieui Hoi,* meaning "Welcome Back" or "Open Arms," which began in 1964. One of the motion pictures used in this program was called *The Leaflet.* Acted largely by Viet Cong defectors, it depicted the anguish and disillusionment of a young guerrilla as he killed innocent people. The documentary film ended happily as he presented a surrender pass and was welcomed by South Vietnamese soldiers.

One of the most moving leaflets of 1965 was a poem found on the body of a young North Vietnamese soldier. It was addressed to his mother and described his homesickness and feelings of guilt over killing people like himself in South Vietnam. Leaflets reproducing the poem and identifying the youth and his mother were rained from the air. Several defectors had copies of it.

Most of the South Vietnam leaflets were printed in Saigon, which was headquarters for the 6th Psychological Battalion from Fort Bragg. The battalion also had detachments in each of the corps areas. It usually printed, loaded, and distributed about eighteen million leaflets a week. Less urgent leaflets were produced in Manila, and still others were turned out by U.S. Army Broadcasting and Visual Activity Pacific on Okinawa. The Bragg-trained

7th Psychological Operations Group was stationed there.

The Viet Cong also produced leaflets. They distributed them at night by hand, slipping them under doors, affixing them on walls, or forcing them at gunpoint on surprised villagers. While our leaflets accused the North Vietnamese of being "lackeys of the Communists," theirs termed the South Vietnamese "lackeys of the Americans."

Some English-language leaflets urging our soldiers to quit fighting were strewn around U.S. installations. Some were illustrated with pictures of antiwar demonstrations in American cities. These puzzled and angered some soldiers, but the enemy leaflets as a whole were so crude that they had no effect.

". . . All My Friends Are Dead"

13 SOME OFFICER described the war in Vietnam as "days of protracted boredom punctuated by moments of sheer terror," but I did not find it so. There was always something to do, especially for medics. Initiative and ingenuity were encouraged at Camp Hardy and at many others. Nearly everybody was crossing dates off on girly calendars or otherwise counting the time remaining of his tour, which had been upped from six months to a year toward the end of 1964, but most of us awoke each morning with a cheerful curiosity about what the day would bring. We had little time for brooding or boredom.

One day a new beret patch was ordered for the Fifth Special Forces. The old black shield with a white border, which struck some people as rather mournful, was brightened up by the addition of slanting red and yellow stripes. These are the national colors of South Vietnam.

About the same time, an order came down saying Special Forces men should not roll up their sleeves. When sleeves were rolled up, as they usually were in the hot weather, the bottom stripes, indicating what rank sergeant you were, frequently were concealed. This probably caused some general to have difficulty in distinguishing his chiefs from his Indians, and the order resulted. It was obeyed when visitors arrived but generally ignored otherwise. You had to roll up your sleeves to make bricks or treat the sick.

Camp Hardy continued inviolate as far as the enemy were concerned, but they were all around us, and in in-

creasing numbers, terrorizing and burning villages. The
Special Forces Camp at Plei Me, to the west, where the
"A" team was led by Captain Ronnie Mendoza of Los Angeles and Lieutenant Chuck Barnett of Batesville, Arkansas, beat off an attack in force. The camp at Du Co, to
the northwest on Highway 19 close to the Cambodian border, was besieged at intervals.

A patrol led by Lieutenant Walker and Sergeant Billy
Johnson flushed some of the enemy one day in April just
over the nearest big hill, something we called Mortar
Mountain. Soldiers gave names to everything in Vietnam,
but most of them never made the maps. There was a sharp
fight, and most of the invaders fled. Though surrounded
by our people, one man held his ground and continued
shooting.

The Viet Cong and their North Vietnamese supporters
are cruel and treacherous and inflict unspeakable tortures
on their own people, but some of them are quite brave.
They may choose death instead of surrender. One fellow
once held up a whole American company, throwing rocks
after his ammunition was exhausted, until killed. The soldier trapped by Lieutenant Walker's patrol was of the
same sort.

After he had been killed by a shot from a Montagnard's carbine, he was discovered to be a North Vietnamese army officer, the first we had seen. He was carrying
a rough map of Camp Hardy showing the locations of our
Montagnard companies. The captains of these were also
listed but not in the proper locations. There were marks

on the map indicating a possible attack plan. It caused us to change some of the defenses and hold a lot of practice alerts.

Chief Hoan telephoned us about 11 P.M. a week or so later from his village west of the camp to say that a sizable force of Viet Cong were moving toward us. He gave their precise position. We laid down a barrage of mortar fire there, and Chief Hwan reported that our shots were landing right in the middle of them. When Lieutenant Walker and I went there the next morning, we found no casualties, but the grass had been trampled, and there were bloodstains, indicating that at least some dead or wounded had been dragged away.

We had still another scare when an informer came in with the word that two thousand Viet Cong were marching on Camp Hardy. "If you aren't attacked tonight," he added for emphasis, "you can cut off my head."

This moved several of us to get off what we feared might be our last letters home, but we were not exactly terror-stricken. By then we had all fired our weapons and had been shot at many times. The first time you go into combat, you're scared. You wonder, Will I freeze? Can I function? When you find that you can respond, it is a great relief, a great satisfaction. You laugh, you yell, you celebrate.

A soldier doesn't worry too much about the bullet with his name on it—that's fate, and there can't be many of them. But he spends a lot of time worrying about those bullets just addressed "To whom it may concern."

My real fear was of being taken alive. I'd rather go all at once than to have them take me apart slowly.

Fortunately, Camp Hardy was not attacked. If there were two thousand Viet Cong afoot, they passed us in the night. We were so happy about it that despite the informer's invitation, we did not bother to cut off his head. Some other camps were not so lucky.

Several members of the B-20 Special Forces team with which I came to Vietnam were shifted from Kontum far south to a camp at Song Be, a provincial capital near the Cambodian border and seventy-four miles north of Saigon. These included Staff Sergeant Horace Young, who had been at the farewell party at Bragg with his Japanese wife, Major Sakey, Sergeant Major Robert Frander, and Sergeant David Charles Crockett. They were part of a thirty-two-man team, the senior officer of which was Lieutenant Colonel Alton E. Park of Columbus, Georgia. With them were two hundred South Vietnamese Rangers.

A force of around two thousand Viet Cong hit Song Be on the dark night of May 10–11 and attacked the camp with guns, grenades, and mortars. In the first five minutes of an hour-long battle, Colonel Park and a dozen others were wounded and placed in the mess hall, where the medic, Sergeant William F. Benning, with Sergeant Lauren Green, attempted to take care of them. But the Viet Cong tossed in grenades and then broke into the mess hall, wounding Colonel Park again and killing Sergeant Benning and two of the wounded, Lieutenant Henry A. Deutsch of Greenville, South Carolina, and Specialist-4 Amos C. Watson of Wilson, North Carolina. Sergeant John K. Culbreath of Callison, South Carolina, was killed as he ran from his foxhole to the mess hall in an effort to protect the wounded.

They found my friend Sergeant Young dead, spread-eagled on a bloody pantry door clutching a penknife. Wounded earlier by mortar fragments, he had been lying on the mess-hall floor, when a grenade was tossed through the door. He attempted to push it out with the barrel of his empty rifle, but the grenade exploded, tearing his arm. Crazy with pain, Young grabbed at a figure in the dark. It was Specialist-4 Gige Kelso of Alton, Illinois.

"It's a friend," whispered Kelso. He wiped the blood off Young's face and neck.

"Let's get some weapons," said Young.

He then struggled with and apparently stabbed a youthful Viet Cong who had broken into the building. The latter fled trailing blood. Young then collapsed and bled to death amid cans of tomato juice.

Though wounded repeatedly by grenade and mortar fragments, Sergeant Major Frander and Sergeant Crockett got a machine gun going and the Viet Cong were driven out, leaving fifty-nine of their dead behind. There were forty South Vietnamese killed. I included Sergeant Young's name in my song "I'm a Lucky One." Besides his widow, he left two small sons.

At this time, on the basis of experience, the Special Forces adopted a new policy on replacements. Instead of replacing one entire team with another, new men would be brought in individually or a few at a time so that each camp would always have some veterans who knew the area well. Some teams previously had taken over a camp after only a week's orientation.

Under this system, Camp Hardy received some new officers, Captain John Rave and Lieutenants Hunt and Hudson. To replace Sergeant Wright, the weapons man who had moved to a camp near Da Nang, we received young Staff Sergeant Raymond Vrba, Jr., from the Special Forces camp at Dong Tre. The emphasis on team operation continued. Every man was supposed to know each member of the team by name and voice to prevent any mix-ups in darkness or emergencies.

Sergeant Vrba was only twenty-two years old but a fine soldier. He had been born in Waco, Texas, and graduated from Reicher High School. He was a devout Catholic and had been an altar boy and a Cub Scout. Because his father was a chief warrant officer, the family had lived in many states and in Germany, Italy, and Austria. Raymond trained at Fort Hood in Texas and at Benning and Bragg. While at Bragg, he married Linda Hughes, a student at East Carolina College.

Because the newest arrivals were assigned to the hole, Vrba and I shared the same underground sleeping quarters at Camp Hardy. I also took him on his first patrol at Plei Do Lim. It was a five-day patrol. We had no fights but picked up a few prisoners and also a boy of about fourteen or fifteen from a Viet Cong village. He admitted having a brother who was a Montagnard VC, but the youngster struck me as being okay. I took him back to camp with me after the patrol. When I ate, he ate. When I slept, he slept. I put him to work in the dispensary. He couldn't count past his fingers and knew nothing about money, but I gave him enough for cigarettes.

"You can go back to your village anytime," I told him after a few days.

"No," he said, "the VC would kill me. I like it here."

So he remained and eventually became a member of our strike force. He was a good boy, and I sometimes wished I could take him back to the United States with me.

We used wood in camp for both fuel and fortification. A woodcutting detail that we had sent south with some of our precious trucks was ambushed by the Viet Cong one day in May. When word of this was called to camp, a reaction force of about ninety Montagnards, under Lieutenant Hudson and Sergeant Vrba, rushed to the scene.

I laid out plasma in the dispensary to be ready for casualties. Shock is the major cause of serious malfunction or death in the field. Plasma and dextran are just as good as blood for preventing shock, and you don't have to bother typing the wounded man's blood. We had no facilities for storing blood at Camp Hardy.

Quite a fight developed as the reaction force reached the trucks. Puff the Magic Dragon, a bullet-spitting old C-47, and flare planes got into the action, which was in the early evening, making it visible back in camp. Soon the casualties began to arrive. Several Montagnards and young Sergeant Vrba had been killed.

I had the task of identifying Vrba's body and shipping it out, along with his personal belongings. Everybody was sad. As Lieutenant Walker said, "Vrba was a damn fine soldier." His wife gave birth to a son, Raymond Vrba III, in Fayetteville a few days later and was unable to attend the burial of her husband at Fort Sam Houston National Cemetery in San Antonio. Raymond's high school in Waco dedicated a new flagpole to his memory at its homecoming football game in 1966.

A remarkable thing about Vrba's death was what happened to his weapon, an AR-15. He was killed at the edge of the action, and the enemy carried off the gun. It was recovered from the body of a Viet Cong killed up at Du Co later. It was taken out then by a Special Forces sergeant. He was killed the next day, and the Viet Cong again captured the AR-15, an incredibly unlucky weapon for all who had handled it.

Vrba is in my song "I'm a Lucky One," along with Young and Horn.

One of those seriously wounded with the reaction force was Chan, the nineteen-year-old interpreter. It was his first patrol. He was shot through the right eye. The Montagnard medic with the party had taken such good care of him that I could only check the eye again and give him morphine for the pain.

"I'm going to lose my eye, *bac-si*?" he asked.

"Yes, I'm sorry to say you are going to lose your eye," I answered.

"Can you get me another—a glass one?"

"Yes."

"Can I come back and work here?"

"Yes."

Chan was evacuated out but recovered and did come back to work wearing a new glass eye!

Lieutenant Hunt and I ran into the Viet Cong south of Plei Do Lim with a patrol a week later. We had no machine guns, but they had two, indicating that there were at least two companies of them. Firing mortars, we pulled back our patrol and got back to camp with the loss of only one man, a Montagnard. He was a local tribesman, and his family mourned him loudly, weeping, screaming, and literally scratching and tearing their faces. It was part of our contract with the Montagnards that their dead be returned for burial in tribal cemeteries.

A few days afterward, I was in the hospital, and my soldiering in Vietnam ended.

The Ballad

14 MOST SOLDIERS who have been patients there have pleasant memories of Clark Air Force Hospital. It was a big, beautiful, modern, air-conditioned place. A band often played as wounded men evacuated from Vietnam were unloaded from airplanes.

"Somebody very important arriving?" one of the soldiers would ask.

"Yes, you," was the answer.

This worked wonders for morale, gave some discouraged men a new interest in life, and undoubtedly helped them recover from their injuries.

After the gash in my leg was sewed up, I was allowed to limp into nearby rooms and visit other patients. One door away, I found an incredible Green Beret, Sergeant Major George A. Vidrine of Port Arthur, Texas. He had suffered a serious *punji* wound in preventing a Marine first sergeant from falling into a Viet Cong pit. A big, burley man, George had served in World War II and Korea, and I had known him in the Seventh Special Forces at Bragg. He had a chestful of medals and later was wounded again, when a helicopter was shot down, to give him a total of seven Purple Hearts while continuing on active duty!

When a little troupe of USO entertainers, pretty girls, sang in the hospital, George demanded that I get out my guitar and sing "The Ballad." I did so and also sang "Bamiba," which I had written in Nha Trang. The title is the name of a potent local beer and literally means

"Three-ten-three." If you drink it, you remember it. Some of my lines go:

> I didn't mean to be drunk
> And bring you all this shame,
> But I had a fight with a cyclo girl
> Down in old Nha Trang.
> It was Bamiba, Bamiba, Bamiba, wa-oh,
> Bamiba, Bamiba, Bamiba, wa-oh.*

These drew more applause than the USO troupe's songs from the men in the hospital. The applause was very good for my morale, and I felt better about my songs.

And speaking of beer, all Filipino troops in Vietnam receive free beer, the gift of the Manila brewery that started the custom for the Filipino force that fought in Korea.

George returned to Vietnam, and I was evacuated to the States. It was about a nine-hour flight in a light jet by way of Japan to Travis Air Force Base, near San Francisco. We were put up overnight in the hospital there, and I telephoned my wife.

"Honey," she asked, "where are you calling from?"

She almost jumped through her hat when I said San Francisco. I told her to get herself down to Bragg. She had her sister's husband, Dale Rabenold, drive her from Lehighton to Fayetteville and got there the day before I did. I was put on a sort of a shuttle plane that flew from station

* Copyright © 1965 and 1966 by Music Music Music Inc.

to station dropping off men near their posts or homes and had to wait two days in New Jersey for a plane to Bragg.

I weighed 190 pounds when I went to Vietnam. I came back weighing 140. My cheeks were sunken, my eyes looked different. My hair was cropped short, and I wore oversize pajamas. Lavona did not recognize me when she first came into the ward at Womack Army Hospital. But I improved rapidly. They let me out to spend nights with Lavona at the guest house, and I returned to Womack for treatments during the day.

It was obvious that the leg would keep me from getting back into the field and that I'd likely spend the rest of my enlistment at Bragg. Lavona proposed that we quit paying rent and buy a house. I agreed. Salesmen took her around, and she picked out a one-story ranch type in Ponderosa, a development down Bragg Boulevard from the post. We signed up for it without my seeing it. Two weeks later, about the end of July, I went on convalescent leave. We drove to Leighton so that I could see Thor, then I went to see my music people in New York.

"The Ballad" was still unsold, but public interest in the Green Berets was increasing. In part this was due to a best-selling fiction book, "The Green Berets," by Robin Moore, a writer both Chet Gierlach and Miss Fairbanks knew. They proposed that we make "Beret" plural in the title of the song and work out some tie-ins with Moore.

They had already arranged one. In an effort to sell my song, they had had The Hunters, John Ireson, Weyman Parham, and Verl Pennington, cut a demonstration record of it. They were selling fifteen hundred of these records at cost to Avon, which was to publish the paperback edition of the Moore book, for a sales convention in Las Vegas. They hoped this would get something going for the song.

Miss Fairbanks heard that Avon was having trouble finding a cover picture for their edition and telephoned John Letheren, an executive there. "I have a real trooper here," she told him. "Why don't you take a look at him?"

He did and sent me to Lester Krauss, the photographer. He made some color shots of me in my green beret. One was used, at first unidentified, on the soft-cover edition of the book. I received $50 as a model's fee. A lunch date was set up for me a few days later with Moore, who had heard the song and was interested in meeting me.

In the meantime, Gierlach listened with interest to the new tapes that I brought him of "Salute to the Nurses," "I'm a Lucky One," and some others. He had missed the program but had heard favorable comments when WABC-TV had used the film of me singing "The Ballad" in Saigon.

"You have a strange and interesting voice," he said. "I think we should push you as a singer as well as a writer."

He had thought of me until then principally as a writer because of the poor technical quality of the earlier tapes. He rented a good guitar for me, and I made some new tapes at once at the Gotham Recording Corp. studio on West Forty-sixth Street.

While there I wrote four new songs, one "The Badge

of Courage," a tribute to the Medal of Honor winners in
Vietnam. The first was Captain Roger H. C. Donlon of
Special Forces. It was awarded next to Sergeant Larry S.
Pierce of the 173rd Airborne Brigade, who was killed when
he threw himself on an exploding mine to save his com-
rades. Private Milton L. Olive, a Chicago Negro boy who
was killed the same way, received the next. The fourth
went to First Lieutenant Charles Q. Williams of the Fifth
Special Forces, who was wounded at Dong Xoai. Later
winners were Specialist-5 Laurence Joel, First Lieutenant
Walter J. Marm, Specialist-4 Daniel Fernandez, and Second
Lieutenant Robert J. Hibbs.

Robin Moore invited me to lunch at the New York
Athletic Club. He had been born Robert L. Moore, Jr., the
son of an organizer of the Sheraton Corporation. He had
given up an executive job with the hotel chain and had
changed his first name to pursue a writing career. To obtain material for his Green Beret book, he had gone to
jump school and by special permission had taken courses
at Bragg. He had been a staff sergeant in the Air Force
during World War II.

He moved me from the small West Side hotel where I
was staying to a suite at the Sheraton East. When I mentioned I needed a good guitar, he bought me a $140 instru-
ment in an Eighth Avenue pawnshop that afternoon. In return for half of my interest in the song, he wrote a new
third verse, added his name, and agreed to do all he could
to sell it. He began by calling in his friend Bob Considine,
who wrote two syndicated columns about me.

I had been adding and discarding verses to "The

Ballad" for two years. At one time there were fifteen verses. But many were too obscure, too dated, or otherwise not right. Robin's lines, most people agreed, added interest and controversy. I made some new tapes including two of Robin's lines that gave me the idea for these verses:

> Back at home a young wife waits.
> Her Green Beret has met his fate.
> He has died for those oppressed
> Leaving her his last request:
> Put silver wings on my son's chest.
> Make him one of America's best.
> He'll be a man they'll test one day.
> Have him win the Green Beret.*

Robin and Chet introduced me at William Morris, the talent agency that represented Robin, Maurice Chevalier, Tony Martin, Sammy Davis, Jr., and many others. Some people there liked my tapes very much. They signed me instantly. Robin and I thought this took care of everything, and he went off to Vietnam to write a series of articles for the Hearst newspapers.

I picked up Thor and Lavona in Lehighton. We attached a U-Haul to the car for the drive to Fayetteville. Her family had given us some furniture and we had bought some more for our new house, all very modest items. At Bragg, they assigned me to a job in the surgeon's office and, as my leg improved, as an instructor in hand-

* Copyright © 1966 by Music Music Music Inc.

to-hand combat. In November I made a trip to Colorado to see my mother and brother, and Lavona went to work as a nurse's aide in the Cape Fear Valley Hospital at Fayetteville.

The William Morris Agency, despite its size and prestige, was unable to do anything with my songs. I may have been too little and too unknown. But "The Ballad" continued to be praised and played around Bragg by outfits like the Seventh Special Forces drum-and-bugle corps.

I asked Chet Gierlach how much it would cost to press a few hundred records of it. With only a small orchestra, he said, it would be about $750. I undertook to raise the money among my fellow sergeants at Bragg and began to take pledges.

Meanwhile, one of Robin Moore's friends, Clancy Isaac of Maplewood, New Jersey, invited Robin to speak at the annual meeting of the Maplewood Civic Association. On his return from Vietnam, Moore kept the date, waiving his lecture fee, on the evening of November 18.

Clancy had Robin, Robin's brother John, some Civic Association officers, and a few others at his home on Woodhill Drive after the meeting. Robin there told Clancy, an ebullient marketing man, about "The Ballad of the Green Berets." Clancy agreed to call RCA Victor, where he had often discussed the marketing of records, and try to obtain a hearing for it. He then flew off for the weekend to see Ohio State defeat Michigan at football in Ann Arbor. This game, I learned, was an annual ritual for Clancy. His father had been a coach and he had been a cheerleader at Ohio State. He had served in the Pacific in World War II and had risen from private to major.

When Clancy returned on Monday, John Moore reminded him of his promise, and he telephoned Dick Broderick, an RCA Victor executive. Broderick agreed to listen to the songs, saying they were always looking for talent and particularly someone who might fill the void created by the untimely death in an airplane crash of Jim Reeves. Chet Gierlach delivered all the tapes to Broderick. As they say in the industry, Broderick "had ears" and convinced Irwin Tarr, Joseph D'Imperio, and Harry Jenkins, RCA vice-presidents, that this was the right tune, right place, and right man with the right song. Overnight RCA decided they wanted both the songs and the singer. Chet telephoned me that day, November 24, the day before Thanksgiving, 1965.

"We are going to save the sergeants their money," he said. "RCA Victor wants you to record an album."

"Are you sure?" I asked.

He was. By luck and chance, I had gotten in five days what I had been seeking for more than two years. They wanted me to come to New York as soon as I could get leave. I sent a telegram canceling my William Morris contract and got to New York on December 2.

I signed a recording contract in Dick Broderick's office that morning, was given a $500 advance, and went over my songs with Andy Wiswell, the RCA artists-and-repertoire man. Broderick had been an Army lieutenant in the Reserve, and his first sergeant was a young man named Victor Catala. We were introduced, and I decided we sergeants should stick together, so that afternoon I signed a management contract with Catala. Catala managed a number of show-business people. I spent the night with Chet and his actress wife, red-haired Ann Thomas, at their home on Highbrook Avenue in Pelham, New York, and telephoned Lavona the good news.

Wiswell wanted four more songs for the album. I flew back to Fayetteville, wrote five in two days, and sent him the tapes. RCA Victor had a sheaf of sixteen songs from which to choose twelve. They wanted to record a day or two earlier, but I couldn't get to New York until Saturday, December 18.

The weather had delayed planes. Instead of getting in the night before, as planned, I arrived early Saturday morning. It was a cold, blustery day. After only an hour's sleep, I got up and went over the material with Chet. I'm not a composer as far as writing out music for all the instruments. I can't really write a note. But I can supply the bones of a song, words and music on tape, and others can put the meat on them, fill them out, make them walk. Andy Wiswell had employed Sid Bass, a great free-lance arranger, to do this for mine.

We began to record at noon in Studio A at the RCA Victor Building on East Twenty-fourth Street. The company had provided a fifteen-piece orchestra and a male chorus. I had never worked with so many people before.

I first sang "Lullaby," one that I had written in a few minutes for my son, Thor. It begins "Go to sleep, it's getting late, my watch says it's half-past eight." This went smoothly. Next came "Letter from Vietnam," "I'm Watching the Raindrops Fall," and "Badge of Courage." By then it was 2:30 P.M., and we took a break.

"The Ballad of the Green Berets" began the next session. There was a stir among the musicians and also among the RCA executives outside the glass as I launched into the familiar-to-me lines:

> *Fighting soldiers from the sky,*
> *Fearless men who jump and die,*
> *Men who mean just what they say,*
> *The brave men of the Green Beret.*

This was followed by "Bamiba," the beer song, and "Saigon," which was the only one with which I had trouble. We had to do about twenty retakes on one note that I couldn't seem to get right. But this and "Salute to the Nurses" as well were completed by 6 P.M.

We went to dinner at La Strada East, a fine Italian restaurant around the corner on Third Avenue. On Andy Wiswell's urging, I ate their Chicken Gellis, and it justified his praise. Several people made guesses as to what the sales would be of the single record "The Ballad of the Green Berets" and of the twelve-song album. Some conservatives mentioned fifty thousand to eighty thousand. Wiswell was sure "The Ballad" would do better than

"Bridge Over the River Kwai." Others were confident that both the single and the album would be top sellers.

Between dinner and 11 P.M., we recorded "I'm a Lucky One," "The Soldier Has Come Home," "Trooper's Lament," and "Garet Trooper." I then went to bed.

When the single was released January 11 and the album January 20, sales of both took off like wildfire. In Fayetteville, I autographed eighteen hundred singles in four hours at a Sears Roebuck store for the benefit of a Bragg charity fund. Outlets ordered and reordered, and both the single and the album climbed to the peak of the top-tune lists and stayed there a long time. In Pelham, New York, Mrs. Gierlach framed an album cover over the bed in her guest room and put up a sign that read: "Barry Sadler slept here."

There were stories about the songs in most newspapers, in *Life, Time,* and *Newsweek,* and in *Variety, Billboard, Cash Box,* and other music magazines. United Press International and the Associated Press interviewed me. Some antiwar students at the University of Minnesota added to the attention "The Ballad" received by protesting the playing of it on the air. Within a few weeks, I sang on television programs on all the networks. I was on *The Ed Sullivan Show, The Jimmy Dean Show,* an NBC *Home Front* program about Vietnam, and Martha Raye's ABC-TV *Hollywood Palace* program.

On the Martha Raye show, I received two record-industry gold records, marking the sale of more than a million copies of both the single and the album. It was the first time in years that a singer received two gold records at the same time. Sales of the single passed two million in five weeks. I gave one of the replica gold records to Lieutenant Colonel Eugene Mills, an information officer at Bragg who had been a friend of my father in New Mexico and who gave me good advice as to how to deal with my good fortune. I gave one to Clancy Isaac, whose telephone call had proved so lucky, and put the other on the wall at home.

At Bragg, I was moved into the Public Information Office. It sorted out requests for my appearance and scheduled me for patriotic meetings and recruiting rallies across the country. I made a trip to the Canal Zone. At times I shared platforms with Vice-President Hubert Humphrey, former Vice-President Richard Nixon, Secretary of Defense McNamara, Secretary of State Rusk, Miss America, Governor George Romney of Michigan, Governor John A. Volpe of Massachusetts, and many others. I collected all sorts of scrolls, keys to cities, and other awards. In San Francisco, my nurse friend Lieutenant Colonel Margaret Clarke and I appeared together at a recruiting rally and talked about Nha Trang. She became chief nurse at Noble Army Hospital at Fort McClellan, Alabama. On a trip to Fort Huachuca, Arizona, I saw my Grandfather Littlefield and some of my aunts and cousins for the first time in years.

An editorial in the Goldsboro, North Carolina, *News-Argus* predicted a long life for "The Ballad," saying: "The Vietnam war has produced a song which will live long. It will live as long as 'Long, Long Trail,' 'White Christmas,' or any that you can name. . . . Already it has captured the heart of the nation and is deepening and thrilling the patriotic feelings of millions. . . . 'Ballad of the Green Berets' causes chills to run up and down your spine. It has a mournful note that makes you see and feel war in all its strangeness."

In New Jersey and elsewhere, it was played over loudspeakers as a reply to antiwar demonstrations. It helped create a boom in Green Beret products. Women as well as Girl Scouts began to wear them. It was made a trademark for soaps and toiletries. Sears Roebuck and other mail-order catalogs appeared in 1966 with pages of Green Beret toys.

At least fifteen other artists recorded "The Ballad" in the United States, and I shared in the royalties. These included Teresa Brewer, Kate Smith, Paul Lavalle, Johnny Paycheck, Ray Anthony, Arthur Fiedler, and other well-known names. It was published in sheet music and in piano rolls, roll-around tape, and tape cartridges.

More than forty recordings were issued under RCA and other imprints in other countries. It was sung and published in sheet music in Dutch, German, Spanish, Japanese, Italian, Swedish, Finnish, French, and perhaps other languages. The East Germans gave it some worldwide publicity by banning it. All translations were reasonably close to my words except the French. Vietnam is an unpleasant memory in France. There Louis Amade gave the tune entirely different words, and it was retitled "Passeport Pour le Soleil" ("Passport to the Sun").

All concerned naturally profited beyond our wildest

hopes. Gerald Gitell used part of his share to buy his elder brother Herbert a Dunkin' Donuts franchise in Framingham, Massachusetts. Gitell had served at three camps in Vietnam, at one taking the place of Lieutenant Royal G. Isaacs, who had been killed. As this is written, Gitell is a civilian employee of the Army in Washington, D.C., and lives in Arlington, Virginia.

Lavona and I paid off our mortgage. I bought a color-television set, a few World War II weapons and other souvenirs, some cameras and a telescope that I had been wanting. Our only extravagances were two Jaguars, a black one for me and a blue one for her. While back in Pennsylvania on a visit in 1966, she drove her car into the drive-in restaurant where she had worked while I was in Vietnam. Everybody was glad to see her. "You can laugh at everybody now," said James Minnich, the proprietor, "and buy yourself a house with pillars."

I visited hospitals across the country and sang in many of them. Among others, I especially remember the young patients at the Variety Children's Hospital in Florida and at the Crippled Children's Hospital in Springfield, Massachusetts, as well as the veterans in Fitzsimons General Hospital in Denver.

A lot of newspapermen interviewed me, one of them over a cup of coffee. He asked whether I could write a song about it. I replied, "You and me, a cup of coffee, recalling things that used to be. . . . I wonder what will become of me."

Taps

15 I HOPE TO WRITE a song sometime based on taps, the bugle call that signals the end of the soldier's day and sometimes of his life. It is the newest bugle call and the only one for which America can take any credit.

Until the Civil War, we used the French lights-out (*l'extinction des feux*) to mark the end of the day's activities. It was supposed to have been a favorite of Napoleon, but General Daniel Butterfield of the Army of the Potomac didn't like it. He didn't know a note of music, but with the aid of bugler Oliver W. Norton, General Butterfield created taps one July night in 1862 while encamped at Harrison's Landing, Virginia.

That same year, taps sounded at a military burial so close to the front that it was unsafe to fire the traditional three volleys. It was soon adopted and made official throughout the American Army and years later was adopted by the French Army as well. Various words have been written, including these:

> Fades the light,
> And afar
> Goeth day,
> Cometh night;
>
> And a star
> Leadeth all,
> Speedeth all
> To their rest.

I have more years ahead of me, I hope, than behind me, but my nine-year Army career is ending. I will always look back on it with pride. I cherish the Purple Heart Medal given me one morning in the surgeon's office at Fort Bragg by Lieutenant Colonel Richard L. Coppedge for my *punji*-stick wound. I am proud to be an honorary member of the Special Forces Decade Club, composed of officers and men who have served ten years in the Green Berets.

While I have had bad moments, the Army as a whole has been a great experience for me, with the pluses far outweighing the minuses. When my son, Thor, grows up, I want him to spend some time in the Army. In fact, I'm going to start him on judo and karate by the time he is five.

I want to do many things—write more songs; perhaps open a good restaurant somewhere, maybe in San Francisco; maybe travel across Asia; read a lot of poetry; and perhaps record some albums of the classics. I also want to do something for the children of men who will not come back from Vietnam.

I was lucky enough to come back with only a serious scratch. Most soldiers do. Even in the Special Forces, where 143 men were killed in combat out of a strength of around 1,100, more than four-fifths returned safely. But the remainder, the LeGrands, Youngs, and Horns, often leave children. I would like to help them.

With the encouragement of leaders of the U.S. Junior Chamber of Commerce and the American Legion, whose past commanders gave me their 1966 Favorite Serviceman Award, I have established the Barry Sadler Foundation. The aim is to provide full college scholarships for the children of servicemen of any branch of the military who are disabled in the line of duty. The Foundation's New York State certificate of incorporation reads: ". . . the objects and purposes . . . shall be exclusively charitable, and in furtherance of such objects and purposes the Corporation shall provide financial aid and assistance in the form of grants, awards, and scholarships to qualified children of deceased and disabled enlisted men and officers of all branches of the military forces of the United States of America in connection with the college and other post-secondary school education of such children."

I hope others will open their hearts and their purses and join me in supporting this.

"... My Friends I Left Across the Sea."

Killed in Action with Special Forces, Southeast Asia

NAME	DATE OF DEATH
1. Bischoff, John M.	April 22, 1961
2. Biber, Gerald M.	April 22, 1961
3. Moon, Walter H.	July 22, 1961
4. Gabriel, James J.	April 8, 1962
5. Marchand, Wayne E.	April 8, 1962
6. Cordell, Terry D.	October 15, 1962
7. Fannin, Clayton A.	January 10, 1963
8. Hain, Robert J.	May 6, 1963
9. Brodt, James H.	May 29, 1963
10. MacIver, Neil K.	May 29, 1963
11. Mosier, Robert K.	July 18, 1963
12. Goodman, Jack L.	July 18, 1963
13. Hackley, Lawrence E.	July 18, 1963
14. McBride, Claude W.	August 23, 1963
15. Gribb, Edward B.	August 26, 1963
16. Johnson, James H.	October 3, 1963
17. Everhart, William J.	November 8, 1963
18. Brockman, Verdean A.	November 16, 1963
19. Townsend, Chester D.	December 1, 1963
20. Hardy, Herbert F., Jr.	March 4, 1964
21. Montgomery, William John	May 5, 1964
22. Self, Irving A.	May 19, 1964
23. Gray, Jesse A.	June 12, 1964
24. Walling, Harry A.	June 19, 1964
25. Alamo, Gabriel	July 6, 1964
26. Houston, John L.	July 6, 1964
27. Underwood, George Warner	July 23, 1964
28. Kidd, Dennis C.	August 4, 1964
29. McNeil, Harold L.	August 12, 1964
30. Patience, William Ronald, Jr.	August 21, 1964
31. Towery, Herman	October 22, 1964
32. Sparks, Charles Pierce	October 24, 1964

". . . My Friends I Left Across the Sea."

NAME	DATE OF DEATH
33. Woods, Lawrence	October 24, 1964
34. Toth, William Charles	October 27, 1964
35. Paliskis, Eugene M.	November 16, 1964
36. Horn, Emmett H.	December 23, 1964
37. Siegrist, William L.	December 30, 1964
38. Panula, Reino, A.	December 30, 1964
39. VanAlstine, Merle O.	February 10, 1965
40. Gaffney, Ronald S.	February 19, 1965
41. Rose, Gerald B.	February 22, 1965
42. Chase, Mark R.	March 4, 1965
43. Widder, David J. W.	March 24, 1965
44. Isaacs, Royal G., Jr.	April 23, 1965
45. Bowan, William T.	May 7, 1965
46. Culbreath, Johnie K.	May 11, 1965
47. Young, Horace E.	May 11, 1965
48. Thomas, Murrel D.	May 22, 1965
49. Peters, Lynn W.	May 25, 1965
50. Vrba, Raymond J., Jr.	May 25, 1965
51. Mosher, Maurice W.	May 25, 1965
52. Brainerd, Fleming B., III	May 26, 1965
53. Russell, Bobby	June 10, 1965
54. Jenkins, Charles O., Jr.	June 10, 1965
55. Dedman, Donald C.	June 10, 1965
56. Talley, James L.	June 20, 1965
57. Ledbetter, Thomas	June 20, 1965
58. Stepanov, Robert D.	July 5, 1965
59. Grogan, Bryan E.	July 5, 1965
60. Jimenez, Luis R.	July 10, 1965
61. Kierzek, Stanley P.	July 20, 1965
62. Bradshaw, Faybert R.	July 20, 1965
63. Melton, Clifford D.	July 21, 1965
64. Morgan, David A.	September 23, 1965

NAME	DATE OF DEATH
65. Pruitt, James E.	September 27, 1965
66. DeAmaral, Charles F., Jr.	October 4, 1965
67. King, James H.	October 6, 1965
68. Bailey, Joseph D.	October 20, 1965
69. McBynum, Jimmie L.	October 22, 1965
70. Pusser, Thomas W.	October 22, 1965
71. Hayward, Earnest	October 25, 1965
72. Sapp, Stanley L.	December 4, 1965
73. West, Grayson	December 16, 1965
74. Arnn, John O.	December 26, 1965
75. Torello, Carl H.	December 26, 1965
76. Fewell, John P. Jr.	January 28, 1966
77. Jacobsen, Donald J.	January 29, 1966
78. Cook, Marlin C.	January 29, 1966
79. Dotson, Donald L.	January 29, 1966
80. Hancock, Jesse L.	January 29, 1966
81. Hoagland, George A., III	January 29, 1966
82. Reifschneider, Elmer J.	January 29, 1966
83. Brown, Earl F.	January 29, 1966
84. Badolati, Frank N.	January 29, 1966
85. Wood, William M., Jr.	February 13, 1966
86. Lee, Robert	February 17, 1966
87. Hall, Billie A.	March 9, 1966
88. Allen, Raymond	March 9, 1966
89. McCann, Owen F.	March 9, 1966
90. Taylor, James L.	March 10, 1966
91. Stahl, Phillip T.	March 10, 1966
92. Hughes, James E.	March 13, 1966
93. Parker, Udon	March 13, 1966
94. Scull, John F., Jr.	March 21, 1966
95. Willey, Alden B.	March 27, 1966
96. Donker, Leo M.	April 3, 1966

"... My Friends I Left Across the Sea."

NAME	DATE OF DEATH
97. Shelton, Ronald T.	April 10, 1966
98. Conway, James	April 12, 1966
99. Kasrzyk, Gerald D.	April 23, 1966
100. Baumert, Brent J.	April 26, 1966
101. Michelli, Angelo F.	May 3, 1966
102. Welsh, Thomas R.	May 16, 1966
103. Pellegrino, Joseph D.	May 18, 1966
104. Cherry, J. L., Jr.	May 18, 1966
105. Casey, Maurice A.	May 24, 1966
106. Moore, Nelson R.	May 24, 1966
107. Broome, Cecil A., Jr.	May 26, 1966
108. Casale, James E.	May 29, 1966
109. Baker, Jack A.	June 14, 1966
110. Clements, Lonnie E.	June 20, 1966
111. Schmidt, Donald F.	June 20, 1966
112. Versace, Humbert R.	July 1, 1966
113. Roraback, K. M.	July 1, 1966
114. Will, William A.	July 5, 1966
115. Binion, Curtis E.	July 5, 1966
116. Codley, Warren W.	July 8, 1966
117. Gallant, Henry J.	July 14, 1966
118. Taylor, Fred	July 14, 1966
119. Sain, Don R.	July 29, 1966
120. Pearson, John R.	August 17, 1966
121. Wells, Allen G.	August 17, 1966
122. Majure, Eugene J.	August 18, 1966
123. Harbin, Carl S., Jr.	August 25, 1966
124. Girtanner, Jules T.	August 26, 1966
125. Lehew, Donald L.	August 26, 1966
126. Cunningham, Wells E.	August 27, 1966
127. Moreau, Eugene R.	August 27, 1966
128. Drummond, E. F., Jr.	September 23, 1966

NAME	DATE OF DEATH
129. Borowsdy, C. G.	October 10, 1966
130. Menefee, G. A.	October 12, 1966
131. Sills, Darel L. (Psy Ops)	October 14, 1966
132. Terwilliger, Roger E. (Psy Ops)	October 14, 1966
133. Lennon, Frederick W.	October 17, 1966
134. Jackson, Edward, Jr.	October 17, 1966
135. Vessels, Charles R.	October 18, 1966
136. Lewis, Frederick H.	October 18, 1966
137. Thorne, Larry A.	October 19, 1966
138. Newbern, Michael R.	October 22, 1966
139. Anderson, Boyd W.	October 22, 1966
140. Dunn, Creighton R.	October 29, 1966
141. Mihalek, Adelbert F.	October 30, 1966
142. Finn, James N.	October 18, 1966
143. Boyd, David S.	November 14, 1966